THE VERY SOCIAL BROKER

SOCIAL MEDIA SECRETS & STRATEGIES TO
MAKE YOUR REAL ESTATE BUSINESS EXPLODE

RYAN GARSON

The Very Social Broker Social Media Secrets & Strategies to Make Your Real
Estate Business Explode

Published by
Illumify Media Global
www.IllumifyMedia.com
"Let's bring your book to life!"

Typeset by Jen Clark
Cover design by Debbie Lewis

Printed in the United States of America

CONTENTS

INTRODUCTION

Let's cut to the chase. If you are a real estate agent in the 21st century and you think you can ignore social media...think again.

Social media isn't just for kids anymore. Look at Instagram alone. As of the time of this writing, there are over 1 billion people on Instagram--one-seventh of the world's population. Of those billion, 32.1 percent are between the ages of 25-34. Add those who are 34 and up, and you've got more than 500 million people over the age of 25. That's basically everyone who is a potential home buyer--your entire target market!

If you want to market your brand, you have to go where your target market is and reach out to them. That's Marketing 101.

I'll probably say this several times throughout this book, but repetition reinforces...so let's start now:

If you're a real estate broker who is not using social media to market yourself--you're leaving money on the table. Period.

The modern real estate market is an online one, and if you are not making social media an integral part of your marketing strategy yet, your competitors will soon be eating your lunch.

You're Doing It Wrong

If you are already on social media, you're probably trying to make the most of things, but if you're like most brokers, you're probably getting frustrated with the process. It is easy to lose interest in social media marketing when your results are not as strong as you would like them to be.

But that doesn't mean social media doesn't work. It just means you're doing it wrong.

When you do it right, social media is a powerful tool to boost your client base and sales significantly through word-of-mouth publicity, which can also help bring more buyers into the offline world later on. People are turning to social media (especially Instagram) for all sorts of things, including making buying and selling decisions. And the more you use social media effectively and strategically, the greater your chances of success will be in real estate.

But...how?

I'm glad you asked.

I started in the New York City real estate market five years ago as a newcomer to the city with no experience and no connections. For the first two years, I spun my wheels, watching with frustration as the other more seasoned agents sold circles around me. Then, I tapped into some social media techniques that changed my entire approach to real estate marketing and branding. In a fairly short period of time, I went from selling almost nothing to selling millions of dollars a year in real estate. I now oversee a team of five agents and my own social media company, and social media is a cornerstone of our marketing process. My success has been so profound that other agents are now seeking me out, begging to know my secrets.

And that's why you're now holding this book.

What You Can Expect

In the pages ahead, I'm going to teach you all the best techniques I've learned for leveraging social media to your advantage, and how you can use these techniques effectively to turn your real estate business around. In fact, I think it's safe to say that if you follow even half of the advice in this book and do so systematically, your business will explode.

I'm going to begin by giving you a crash course on social media marketing in general before diving deeper into how you can use it strategically to develop your brand. Whether you're a social media novice or a longtime veteran, there are some crucial lessons I'm going to cover that will take your understanding and use of social media and raise them to the next level.

A Long-Term Strategy, Not a Quick Fix

Let me be clear. Although social media can bring satisfactory results quickly, it's not a magic bullet. Some people try to use it that way, and it never works. I've you've been doing social media for more than a few months, you have probably learned that there are people out there who have thousands of followers, but their posts aren't compelling or valuable. In fact, they may be spammy or even fraudulent. You probably started out following those people on social media, but then you unfollowed them because you didn't want to get caught up in all the "nonsense."

That's definitely NOT what I'm talking about.

Social media isn't a quick-fix solution--it's a long-term strategy that will give you lasting success. Ordinary social media marketing is about growing a following on one or more platforms and then sending those people to your website or landing pages as potential customers through paid advertising.

This book is about something different: it is about attracting and developing a strong and loyal following to promote your brand and services for free.

How to Use this Book

I've tried to structure this book not just as a how-to, but as a long-term resource. Social media is always changing, and the platforms that are popular today may give way to new platforms within a couple of years. However, as someone who has been on social media from the beginning, I can tell you the principles have remained the same: connect with people, engage them, build a following, build trust. Those principles are pretty much the same no matter what platform you use. So even though we'll be talking about effective ways to use specific social media platforms, the strategies I'm about to show you will work across any platform, current or future. You may have to adapt a few things and apply some good old-fashioned trial-and-error--but the principles will still work.

The best way to read this book the first time is to read it from front to back. If you want to get the most value from it, I would recommend reading it a few pages at a time and then pausing to think about actionable steps that you can take to apply what you're learning. That will allow you to digest each concept fully as you go. I personally think that's the best way to make this material your own.

Then, once you've been through the book, hang onto it as a reference manual. When you're working on an Instagram strategy and you need a refresher on your toolkit, re-read the Instagram chapter, for example. If you're struggling to come up with the best hashtags for a post, review the section on hashtags.

I think you'll find this book to be an invaluable resource for your real estate business. The social media strategies I share with you here will save you time and make your marketing much more effective so you can stop spinning your wheels and start making money. If you apply these strategies, you'll soon find that your real estate brokerage is more than just a job...it will become your life.

Let's get started!

1. YOUR NEW SECRET WEAPON

WHEN I WAS 32 years old, I did something that by all accounts would be considered monumentally stupid.

I got my license to become a real estate broker in New York City.

Stupid? you say. *Isn't NYC a pretty hot market for real estate brokers? Aren't the prices of real estate massive there? Aren't the commissions huge?*

Yes. To all the above.

So...why would that be stupid?

Don't get me wrong: NYC is truly one of the best places in the world to sell real estate. But the NYC real estate market is also a much different animal than in other places. It's a huge market with hundreds of unique neighborhoods, mostly condos and co-ops, lots of regulations, lots of red tape, and a massive learning curve. The most successful brokers have lived there for years, know the city like the back of their hand, and built up multiple Rolodexes full of contacts (before, you know, everything went digital). Other successful brokers have at least cut their teeth in other markets for years gaining experience before trying to break into the New York market.

In other words...New York City is great, but it's NOT the

place for someone just starting out in real estate. Unless, maybe, you were born here.

I had none of those things going for me. I was born and raised in Florida. I'd been in the city less than two years and had tried and failed working several jobs before earning my license. I had no experience, I knew almost nothing of the inventory of the NYC market, and I had very few contacts. Launching my real estate career in NYC was not unlike jumping into the deep end of the pool when you've had no swimming lessons.

So, yeah. Stupid.

But that was just my way. I'm an entrepreneur at heart, always have been. When I see the potential to make money, I jump in with both feet. I throw myself into the deep end and start dog paddling until I figure it out.

Over the first two years, it's a wonder I survived. I learned a lot...and sold nothing. I subsisted by brokering rentals while I immersed myself in the market. I looked at every piece of property and every apartment I could, did everything I could to learn the market. But anyone could see what I was up against, including me. The other brokers in my agency had all the advantages I didn't--namely, contacts, knowledge and experience. And they were selling circles around me.

Then, one day, I discovered a secret weapon in my arsenal.

I'd already started utilizing social media to help build my brand, and while I hadn't directly sold much from it, I was gaining at least a modest following. In this instance, I posted an Instagram story about how first-time buyers should go about getting into the market, and someone I'd met five years before at an event reached out to me. We had never been in direct touch after our initial conversation. I followed her on social media, and she followed me, and we liked each other's stuff. She sent me a direct message (DM) on Instagram in response to my story. We set up a phone call, we started talking, and she ended up buying a $3 million apartment from me.

This was when I knew I was really onto something. Here was a person with whom I had very little direct contact, who was not on my mailing list, whose phone number wasn't in my address book, and who never would have thought to call me otherwise. Our only connection was through social media. And that engagement was enough for her to think of me first when she was ready to buy. The amount of money it cost me for that lead: zero dollars.

And the light came on.

I'd grown up with social media, and in fact, I'd used it successfully to grow other businesses I'd had before now. But I hadn't realized how powerful a tool it could be for my real estate career. Suddenly, it was clear: if I could leverage social media correctly, it could put me on the same playing field as other brokers who'd been doing this for years. My *entire target market* was basically sitting here online, millions of people scrolling through their social media accounts several times a day on their phones. If I could get in front of them, engage with them, get them interested in what I was saying and doing...that would be all the contact list I'd need.

It was an epiphany. From that point on, I made social media my primary method for marketing. I treated my Instagram account as my main portal for networking and keeping in touch with prospective clients. It wasn't just about creating great content, engaging people or gaining new followers-- although I did all those things. It was that my *entire mindset changed* about the role of social media in my career.

And it paid off. Big time.

Social media had become my secret weapon.

And once you learn what I'm about to teach you, it can become YOUR secret weapon, too.

But...there's a caveat. For this to work, you have to do more than just glean a few tips, tricks, and techniques to grow your social media. If you approach this book in that way, you will be disappointed with your results, and you'll probably give up. If you want to share in my success, you have to do what I did and *change your thinking* about social media itself and its role in your business. So let's start there.

Dealing with the Skeptics

For many years, there has been a set of accepted marketing tools that real estate brokers are trained to use in order to build their brand and become successful. And not for no reason--at one time or another, every one of these tools has proven useful. The list includes:

- Mass advertising (e.g., newspaper ads, billboards, public transportation ads, TV, radio, real estate magazines)
- Direct mail
- Publishing your listings in local publications
- Cold calling (i.e., "picking up the phone")
- Networking in real life (aka "in-person marketing")

In more recent years with the digital age, we've added email marketing, blogs, and Zillow/Trulia to this list, and in some locations, the use of online MLS listings. We've also put a heavier focus on developing professional websites and using the website as our online business card, so to speak. Trying to get everyone you connect with to go to your website.

Social media has often sat at the bottom of this list. For a long time, it was considered the stepchild of marketing, not on the same level as more traditional forms--at least where real estate is concerned. If you asked a seasoned broker for advice about which marketing tools to use, you'd probably hear something like this: "I'm a traditionalist. I really don't put much stock in social media."

Or perhaps even this: "If people want to find out about me, they can look at my website or call me. Social media is a waste of time and money."

Nowadays, a growing number of agents are utilizing social media as part of their marketing strategy, but for many, it's still a side channel, at best--something they're "supposed" to do because everyone has a Facebook or Twitter account, but not something they view as a legitimate marketing asset. As a result, the excuses keep flying. Maybe you've heard some of these, or even said them yourself:

"Social media isn't a good avenue for selling real estate."

Or,

"Social media is for kids, not homebuyers."

Or my favorite,

"Social media is beneath me."

It's time to face a hard truth. The reason people say these things is not because social media doesn't work. They're saying it because they couldn't get it to work for them. Skeptics like to justify their failures by making excuses.

But where the skeptics are mistaken--and where you may be mistaken--is that social media itself isn't to blame for its own failures to produce results. When something doesn't work for you, it doesn't always mean the method itself doesn't work. It may mean that you didn't know how to use it effectively.

And I can say conclusively that this is the case with social media. The people who say it doesn't work are the ones who haven't figured out how to make it work for them.

Social Media: The New Marketing Landscape for Real Estate Brokers

Now, let's tackle another difficult truth. Remember all the traditional marketing tools I mentioned above?

If you've been in this business a while, have you noticed those tools are not working as well as they used to?

Have you noticed your billboards and direct mailers aren't getting you as many incoming leads? Or that fewer people are calling in from your radio spots?

Again, skeptics like to make excuses, so you're likely to hear (or even say) that the reason these marketing tools aren't as effective is because the market is too crowded (i.e., too many new agents). Or the housing market is down. Or prices are too high. Or this or that or the other thing.

But the truth is...the reason these tools don't work as well is that the public isn't really paying attention to these channels anymore.

The world is changing, and like almost everything else in our world, the real estate marketing landscape is changing, as well. The general public has been so inundated by mass messaging over the past couple of decades that they are basically just tuning a lot of it out. And that includes people who are interested in buying and selling homes--people in your target market.

This is increasingly true of the younger generations-- Millennials and Gen Z-ers--who are just now getting old enough to think about real estate. They listen to mass media even less than the older folks do. And so by going purely the traditional route, real estate agents are pumping thousands of our marketing dollars into media outlets that are being increasingly ignored.

That's why it's not as effective anymore.

But here's the thing. Those people are still out there. And they're still interested in buying and selling real estate. To reach them, you simply have to adjust your approach. You have to invest your time and energy into the outlets they're paying attention to, and put your messaging in front of them. You have to go where they are hanging out.

Any guesses as to where that is?

Yup. Social media.

I want to submit to you that social media IS the new marketing landscape. And it's just as viable for real estate brokers as for any other business out there. In fact, it's becoming more and more vital to your success every day.

A Closer Look at the Numbers

I mentioned in the Introduction that there are currently 1 billion active Instagram users (meaning they use it regularly) and that half of those are over the age of 25. Let's look at a few more numbers just so you can see how much of your target market is actively using social media--and what that means for you:

- *There are currently 3.78 billion people on social media worldwide--more than half the world's population.*[1] This includes a significant percentage of people from all age groups. That number is expected to climb to more than 4 billion by 2025.[2]
- *Seventy-two percent of Americans are currently on social media.*[3]
- *A large percentage of all age groups now use social media (i.e., it's not just for teens anymore).* This includes 81 percent of people in the 30-49 age range, 73 percent of people aged 50-64, and 45 percent of people over age 65.[4] (If you haven't noticed, that's just about everyone who at some point might be thinking about buying a home.)
- *Predictably, 84 percent of people aged 18-29 are on social media.*[4] Don't overlook this group or ignore them, because today's young social media mavens are tomorrow's homebuyers. Any real estate agent who is forward-thinking will be looking for ways to reach this group.

Now, even more exciting than how many people use social media is what they do with it--how they engage. Look at some of the latest data about how consumers have been using social media:

- *Fifty percent of consumers increased their time on social media in the last half of 2020.*[2]
- *Fifty-seven percent of consumers will follow a brand on social media to learn about its new products and services.*[2] (We'll talk more about brand building in later chapters.)
- *Once they've followed a brand, 89 percent of those consumers will eventually buy from that brand.*[2] This is a highly encouraging number, but bear in mind it encompasses buying **all** products--from buying a soda to buying a house. (Not suggesting 89 percent of your followers will buy or sell with you!)

Hopefully, by now you're seeing the potential here. These numbers tell us that almost your entire target market is actively using social media, and if you can find an effective way to use social media to build brand awareness as a real estate broker, you can effectively reach almost all of your potential customers.

This is huge. And this isn't just applicable to real estate; it applies to any brand or company that sells anything, anywhere in the world.

If you want to know why mass media isn't working as well--this is why.

The people you're trying to reach aren't listening to those channels anymore.

They've "changed the channel" to social media. THAT's where they're hanging out.

I'll say it again: if you're ignoring social media as a marketing tool, you're leaving money on the table. The people on social media are the people who will hire you to buy and sell property IF you get yourself in front of them.

I said, "IF."

Why Social Media Isn't Working for You

Remember what I said earlier: If you've tried to use social media and haven't gotten the results you wanted, it doesn't mean social media doesn't work. It just means you're not using it effectively. I can't tell you how many brokers have gotten frustrated over the exact same issue, and how many have dismissed social media as a result. I get it. If you feel like you're wasting your time, the impulse is to chalk up your losses and move on.

Have you ever sat in a flashy sports car with the gear shift in neutral and floored the accelerator? That's how it can feel when you're doing social media wrong. The engine is revving, you can feel and hear all this horsepower, all this promise, all this energy--but you're going nowhere fast.

But it doesn't mean the car doesn't work. You just haven't figured out how to put it in gear.

It's the same with social media. If you don't find the gear that works for you, you'll just sit there and spin your wheels--and if you're like a lot of people, you'll blame the car.

But that's not the problem, is it?

So if that's you, let's talk about some of the most common mistakes real estate agents make--some reasons why you haven't been able to put social media into gear.

You're only using it to promote your stuff.

Many real estate agents have social media accounts they simply use to share their listings. They post a photo of the house and a short description. And that's it until they post again with an updated price or a SOLD sign outside the front door.

Let me ask you a question. Is there anyone you know whom you purposely try to avoid in social gatherings because all they do is talk about themselves? Don't you find that to be a turnoff?

It's exactly the same with social media. By definition, it is SOCIAL. It's not an opportunity for you to talk only about yourself. Nor is it a mass advertising platform. If you treat it as such, people will basically ignore you--for the same reason you ignore the annoying friend at social gatherings. These people are ignoring mass media for a reason. If you only use your social media channel to "sell," you've missed the point. This is one of the biggest issues we'll work to fix in the chapters ahead.

You're not consistent.

If I were to ask people who follow your social media accounts what they've seen from you lately, the answers would probably be: "I'm not sure." or, "Last week he had a bunch of listings posted on his account," or, "He hasn't posted anything in a while."

Lack of consistent posting and engagement on social media is one of the most common issues among real estate brokers. The reasons may be varied, but I think a lot of it stems from a basic misunderstanding of how social media works.

Many people (including agents) have this mindset that you get a bunch of followers on social media, and then every time you post something, everyone on your list sees it. That's not how it works. First, not everyone is online when you post, and second, there are just too many of us on social media for everyone to see everything. Social media platforms have algorithms that prioritize people who are posting regularly. In other words, the more you post, the more you're seen. Consistency of communication is key, especially if you're building a real relationship with your audience.

You're not a real person.

Many agents I've met who are active on social media have a distinctive style that's intriguing to follow, but they don't feel like the people you'd want to hang out with in real life. The vibe is "old school," serious, and somewhat scripted. They post a lot of boring facts about their listings, their business, or the market, but they seldom post about anything personal or human.

This is not the type of friendliness, personality or vibe that you want to present when trying to attract new followers on social media. Success on social media is all about human interaction. People who find you engaging and interesting are far more likely to hire you for a real estate transaction than those who only know about your solid sales record.

You don't have a strategy.

You know that old saying that goes something like, "If you fail to plan, you're planning to fail?" That's definitely true when it comes to social media marketing for real estate. If you want your activity on social media to be effective, there has to be a rhyme and reason behind it. Otherwise, it will feel haphazard and unprofessional--and most importantly, you won't get results.

Having a strategy means that you have a purpose in everything you post, from what you post to how it looks. It means you're engaging in a way that is consistent with your brand-- the type of agent you are and how you want people to see you. We'll talk more in-depth about social media strategies later in the book, but for now, just know that you need one. It takes time and a lot of thought to create a strategy that fits your personality and your goals, but it pays off in the end.

Harnessing the Power of Social Media

Let's go back to the sports car analogy for a minute. All the problems I mentioned above, along with a few others--these are all issues that basically keep you from putting the car into gear. They gum up the works and they keep the engine from engaging. But make no mistake: you're sitting on an extremely powerful machine. Up to now, it hasn't done much for you, but if you are willing to get rid of some of your prior mindsets of social media that are gumming up the works, I can show you in the next few chapters how to put this baby into gear. You'll be amazed at the results.

Before we continue, let me share a bit more about my personal story--how I came across this machine and how I learned to use it to revolutionize my entire real estate business.

2. HOW I DISCOVERED SOCIAL MEDIA MARKETING

AS I MENTIONED EARLIER, I've always been an entrepreneur at heart. I've always been interested in launching new things, seeing opportunities where others don't, and capitalizing on them. That attitude is really what eventually led me to discover the power of social media marketing.

I launched my first business when I was a sophomore in college in Tampa, Florida. I started getting free drink tickets at a local bar in Tampa, and I used them to invite groups of my friends to come. I was in a fraternity, and I started getting everyone to go to the bar using these drink tickets. I was so good at it that the bar eventually started paying me to do it. I wasn't even of drinking age yet myself--I was just happy to be getting into these places--but my ability to gather crowds for a party made me sort of the go-to guy.

Not long after, a new restaurant opened in town, and I went to check it out. I was sitting at the bar, and the owner was sitting next to me. So I said to him, "Hey, this is a great restaurant. You've got a great location and I love the layout. Are you interested in doing events? I could actually bring a couple hundred people here and throw a party every Wednesday night."

"Yeah, that sounds great," he said. "I didn't even think about that."

"Okay, well, why don't you keep the bar, I'll keep the door, and we'll split the expenses?" I asked. He agreed.

So I started the Wednesday night parties. We called it "Eighties for the Ladies." The owner gave me a drink special to advertise, and I went and made fliers and spread the word. I hired a doorman, a DJ, and a couple of security guards from the college football team. I hired a couple of promoters in different fraternities and sororities, and before long, I had 300-500 people showing up every Wednesday night.

That was the start of my first business, Midnight Productions, and we just grew from there. I added a Saturday night party, and I expanded my events to other clubs. I kept this up all through college. By the time I was 21, barely of legal drinking age myself, I had parties happening Tuesday through Saturday in multiple clubs around the Tampa area--as many as 10,000 people coming to my nights on a weekly basis. (It was a great way to go through college, I have to say.)

I quickly found out that one of the best ways to spread the word about my events was through social media. Back then, MySpace was the main platform everyone was using (anyone remember MySpace?), and Facebook was just starting out by expanding from school to school, including mine. I marketed extensively on MySpace, then started some Facebook groups. I learned how to create content that got people interested in what I was doing. These were perfect platforms to use because almost every college kid was on them at that time, and my business was all about engaging people and inviting them to fun events. That early experience showed me the vast potential of using social media to reach people. It was a lesson I never forgot.

After graduating from college, I moved from Tampa to West Palm Beach and started a new business, a pet store called

Palm Beach Puppies. I created a website and started posting videos of myself playing with the puppies. It was highly effective, and I sold puppies all over the country as a result. While this strategy was more on the website side of things, it did show me the power of video marketing, which would eventually merge with social media as it does today.

The Move to New York City

At age 30, I decided it was time for a change. I'd always wanted to live in New York City, so when an opportunity came along, I sold the puppy business and moved to NYC. For the first three months, I ran an event for Tatzu Nishi, an artist who does art installations around public monuments. For this installation, he had set up a living room around the Columbus Statue at Columbus Circle. It was kind of a big deal, and not a bad gig for a newcomer. There were long lines to see the installation every day, a lot of celebrities came to see it, and even the mayor of New York held an event there. When the installation ended, the company that hired me to run it wanted to transfer me back to Florida for another event. I loved New York. I said no and quit.

Over the next two years, I went through six or seven jobs. I was in fashion, I was in hospitality, I was in the event business, I did business development for an experiential marketing agency. Nothing was the right fit. I even got fired a couple of times. During this time, I started going to school to learn real estate and get licensed as a broker, and eventually, I landed a job at a brokerage in the city. I was at a bit of a disadvantage because I hadn't been born and bred in New York, I didn't know a lot of people, and I didn't have a huge Rolodex (remember those?) like other agents did--but the brokerage saw that I loved real estate and they thought I was a go-getter, so they took a chance on me.

In my first two years, I made one sale. I was able to survive because I did a ton of rentals, and I even managed to break the company record for number of rentals. But during that time, I immersed myself in the market. I just learned the business and I was hustling, getting familiar with all the buildings--thousands of apartments in hundreds of buildings throughout NYC.

The A-Ha Moment

Eventually, as I learned the ropes, it became clear that real estate was a great fit for my entrepreneurial mindset. By year three, I started making more sales--even more in year four. I was still on social media, but I was so busy learning the ropes of real estate that I wasn't really mindful of it, nor did I realize its potential to help with my business. So I started to work with a social media strategist to help me out. She was an influencer herself with lots of followers, mainly in the fashion and makeup space. She started posting for me. Her posts didn't feel that authentic, but she was good at getting good photos and getting the copy out there, helping me be consistent with it.

After a year, I switched to another strategist, another influencer who had a bit more experience in real estate. She took my social media to the next level and was great at visuals, doing Instagram stories, and allowing me to connect with my sphere of influence by just helping me provide content that was engaging and looked good.

From that point, I started getting more leads and sales directly from social media. But the real "a-ha" moment for me was still to come.

About this time is when I connected with the Instagram follower I talked about in the previous chapter--the one I'd met five years earlier who responded to my Instagram story. The one who ended up buying a $3 million apartment although I had had no other connection with her except through social media.

This was my "a-ha" moment. But it wasn't as simple as "hey, look what social media did for my business!" What made it a revelation for me was that although it felt random, it wasn't random. This woman didn't magically find me on Instagram and decide out of the blue, "You know what? I'm just gonna drop $3 million here." No. What made it remarkable was that *I had spent five years nurturing this lead and didn't even realize that's what I was doing.* Through consistent engagement on social media, posting interesting content, staying in her feed, I was keeping this lead warm, so to speak. So when she was ready to buy, I was the first person she thought of.

I suddenly saw the true potential of this medium. From that point on, I started leaning more actively into social media as a marketing tool for my real estate business. I took a more active role in building my brand on Instagram. I started focusing on posting better content, not just about my listings, but about life, family, New York City, favorite restaurants, what I was up to, things I love to do--anything that would be of interest to my followers. I made sure my photos and videos looked good and sparked interest. When someone commented or messaged me, I answered them. Posts turned into conversations, and my Instagram became my "newsletter"--my primary way of building brand awareness and mindshare with my audience. People started engaging with my posts--then sharing them. My followers doubled, then tripled.

With this powerful tool now in my arsenal, by year five, my sales really started taking off. Even though I was still relatively new to NYC and didn't have half the connections my fellow brokers had, social media became my connection point, putting me in contact with hundreds of thousands of potential buyers. Thanks to my consistent engagement and brand-building, when many of my followers are ready to buy, sell, or rent in NYC, I'm the guy they think of first. To date, I've sold millions of dollars worth of real estate either directly or indirectly due to social media. I've been able to build my business very quickly without a massive advertising budget. I now have a whole team of agents to help deal with the volume of business.

When I saw how effective social media had been in growing my business, I realized, *every broker needs to be marketing and branding themselves this way.* So in 2019, I started my own social media agency, Very Social, to have a way to help other real estate agents enjoy the same success I had. Very Social serves a diverse roster of clients, but the vast majority of our clients are real estate agents. My social media company now runs alongside my real estate business, and we've got a whole team of creative experts, from copywriters to graphic designers to videographers, who serve the needs of our clients. Very Social is also a preferred partner with the brokerage company I currently work for, and they recommend us to many of their agents.

For decades now, there's been sort of a set formula for how real estate agents market themselves and do brand-building. Conventional wisdom says agents need to market themselves through awareness on billboards, bus stop benches, TV commercials, radio spots, and the like. And those methods still work, but not as effectively as they used to--not to mention the costs involved. But those methods are what I refer to as "old media." Social media is the New Media. One big slogan of mine is that social media today is "The Best Way to Connect." It's where today's buyers and sellers hang out-- young and old, from every income bracket. And when you tap into the best ways to utilize it, it can grow your real estate business at rates you never imagined were possible.

I know there are a lot of skeptics out there. I know there are a lot of agents who still believe social media is not an appropriate or effective platform to sell real estate. But my success from the past couple of years is proof positive that the skeptics are flat wrong. And the best part is, it wasn't dumb luck. Social media works for me because I learned how to work social media. It's a process that can be replicated for any agent who is willing to think differently.

The question is, are you willing? Are you ready to grow your business for real?

3. THE BASICS OF INSTAGRAM FOR REAL ESTATE AGENTS

JUST SO WE'RE CLEAR, the principles and techniques I'm sharing with you in this book are designed to work well within any social media platform. But for our purposes, we're going to spend a lot of time in this book talking about Instagram because it's currently the platform I find the most helpful for real estate brokers. It's also the platform I use most, and it's the one where I've seen the most results. If you can harness the tools of this specific platform and learn to use them well, you'll see a dynamic increase in your following and you'll find brand building much easier. And then, if you like, and as social media evolves, you can carry these techniques to other platforms that you find useful.

From this point forward, I'm operating on the assumption that you have an Instagram account set up. If you don't, stop reading and go set it up. It's free to do. Once you have set up a personal Instagram profile, I recommend converting it to a professional profile (formerly known as a business profile) because doing so unlocks more of Instagram's useful marketing features. (Note: If you don't have a Facebook page for your brokerage yet, you'll need to set one up to convert your personal Instagram profile to a professional profile. Facebook owns Instagram, and it will want to link to your Facebook page. It's a few extra steps, but it's worth it.)

A Quick Overview of Instagram

Instagram began in 2010 primarily as a mobile-based app for taking pictures, adding filters and/or text, then sharing those photos with followers. It has since evolved to incorporate other unique features, but the two things that have always distinguished Instagram from other platforms are that a) it is image-based; and b) it is designed to be used on smartphones. Instagram also includes a suite of on-board editing features and filters so you can edit your photos before posting them--and many users take advantage of these filters to create an overall "look" to their content.

These characteristics make Instagram especially useful for real estate brokers because imagery is a huge part of how we sell homes, plus almost everyone accesses the Internet from mobile devices these days--so with every post, you have an opportunity to engage people immediately with something that is visually appealing.

As with other social media platforms, you have a profile, a feed, people you're following, people who are following you, direct messaging capabilities, hashtag capabilities, etc. But over the years, Instagram has added some more features that can greatly enhance your marketing and branding strategies. These include:

- *Video capabilities.* You can post videos up to 60 seconds long that appear directly in the feed.
- *IGTV.* Short for "Instagram Television," IGTV is a side platform that allows you to post longer videos (up to 15 minutes when posted from your mobile device, and up to 60 minutes when posted from a computer). You can then share a clip up to 60

seconds long on Instagram to entice followers to
click through to the long video.

- *Instagram Stories.* Allows you to post one or more
  quick photos or video snippets that stay online and
  disappear in 24 hours, similar to Snapchat.
- *Instagram Live.* A feature within Instagram Stories
  that lets you broadcast a live video to your
  followers.
- *Instagram Reels.* Sometimes referred to as
  Instagram's version of TikTok, Instagram Reels lets
  you post short videos (between 15 seconds and 30
  seconds long) with creative editing features to help
  make them snappy and engaging. Unlike
  Instagram Stories, Reels don't disappear from your
  profile--but you can share a Reel as an Instagram
  Story.

Anatomy of Your Profile Page

Before we go further, let's do a quick overview of your Instagram profile and how it appears to people who find you there.
We'll talk in detail about to optimize your profile in the next
chapter, but for now, let's just go over the different elements of
your Instagram profile and what they do:

- *Your username.* Shown in large, bold print at the
  top of your profile. (Pro tip: Pick a username that
  is catchy, memorable, and/or gives a clue as to
  what you do. Mine is @ryansellsnyc.)
- *Stats.* Instagram displays the number of posts
  you've created, how many followers you have, and
  how many people you are following.
- *Profile picture.* Currently located on the top left
  corner. A colored ring around your profile pic tells
  visitors you've posted an Instagram Story in the

last 24 hours, and they can click on your photo to
see it.

- *Bio.* Your real name is displayed, followed by a
  small space where you can tell visitors who you are,
  what you do, what you care about, etc. You can
  also provide a URL link here to direct visitors to a
  website, a Linktree, or anywhere else you'd like
  them to visit. (Unlike other platforms like
  Facebook and Twitter, Instagram doesn't allow
  links in posts, so the bio is the only place you can
  put one.)

- *Instagram Story Highlights.* For every Story you
  post, Instagram gives you the option of saving it as
  a Story Highlight so people can revisit it after it
  expires. You can also create multiple categories for
  these Stories. If you're using this feature, your
  Instagram Story Highlights will show up as circular
  icons just below your bio in their respective
  categories.

- *Grid.* Instagram displays a square thumbnail of
  every post you've made (except for any that you've
  archived) in order beginning with the most recent.
  These thumbnails are grouped three across in a
  grid pattern.

Bear in mind that like every social media platform, Instagram is constantly updating and changing things about its
app, so what I've described above may look or feel different
with future updates, or Instagram may add more features, etc.
But for the most part, these elements listed above are likely to
appear somewhere on the page, and you'll want to familiarize
yourself with them because I'll be showing you how to optimize these features a bit later.

How to Turn Instagram Into Your Primary Marketing and Branding Tool

I'd highly recommend taking some time looking around inside Instagram on your own time, getting acquainted with all the tools and resources that are there. We'll go into more depth on how to use many of these tools later in the book. But at this point, I want to introduce you to a different way of approaching Instagram than you've probably imagined or been taught--different than most real estate brokers see it...

I want you to stop looking at social media in general--and Instagram in particular--as just "one more tool in your toolbox."

I want you to envision Instagram as your primary tool. Your main portal for reaching your audience. Your main outlet for marketing and branding. Because when you start looking at it like that, the possibilities are endless.

Think about this for a minute. Consider all the different ways you're currently trying to engage your audience. You've probably got a website. You're probably putting out an email newsletter. Maybe you're doing some mailers. You're meeting people at networking events and talking to them one-on-one. You're handing out business cards.

Now...imagine having all of those possible connection points in one place where your target market hangs out all the time. Wouldn't that be much easier? Could you see the potential of combining all those outreaches in a single platform?

THAT's how I want you to start seeing Instagram.

That's secret number one.

For me, Instagram has essentially become my website, my email newsletter, and my networking space all in one. It's like a website because it's a great branding tool for me, and it's like a newsletter because it's the best way to keep up-to-date with my sphere of influence with my in-feed posts and my Stories.

Don't get me wrong--I have a nice website, I have an

email newsletter, and I still go to networking events. I have business cards. I even do mailers. BUT instead of handing out my cards en masse, trying to get people to subscribe to my email newsletter or pointing them to my website...I just ask them to follow me on Instagram. It's my primary call-to-action--so much so that with virtually every other tool I use to engage people, I include an invite to follow me on Instagram.

I put it on my newsletters.

I put it on my mailers.

I put it on my business card.

I put it at the top of my website, along with my other social media.

I put it on my email signature so it goes out on every email I send.

I mention it when I'm talking to people in person. And if the moment presents itself, I even have the person pull out their phone and follow me right then and there.

Why?

Because it's literally the best and easiest way for people to connect with me and see what I'm up to. It's the easiest way for me to gather all my prospects into one place where I can communicate with them, educate them, and build trust and awareness.

And I do more than just point people to my Instagram; I give them a reason to pay attention. I post a TON of content there.

In fact, it's how I spend the majority of my marketing time. When I'm not actively showing a home or writing up a deal, I'm usually doing something pertaining to social media-- working up content to post, talking to followers on DM, etc. I'm engaging my audience. Constantly.

I spend so much time on Instagram that the skeptics might argue that I spend too much time there. That maybe I'm so consumed with social media that I'm not doing my "job." That I'd make more money if I focused more attention on actually SELLING real estate.

To the critics, I say only this: my revenue suggests otherwise.

Here's my point. If it looks to you like I'm spending too much time on social media, it's because you still have an old mindset that believes social media is something you do on the side. When you start treating Instagram as your main way to engage your audience, build your brand, and get leads...it's not too much time at all.

You see, I don't have any more time than you do. We all have the same amount. It's all about how we budget that time. Any business guru will tell you that the key to being successful is to spend most of your time on the things that are producing results for you.

I spend lots of time on Instagram because that's what's getting me the leads, and ultimately, the sales.

Not my website.

Not my email list.

Instagram.

Again, it's not a matter of either/or. I have those other marketing tools, and I use them. I just use them proportionately to the revenue they are generating for me.

I don't have to hard-sell myself to prospects using those other marketing tools because by using Instagram correctly, my leads are coming to ME. They approach ME when they want to buy or sell because I've invested so much time (and yes, money) to build mindshare with them on their Instagram feed.

Here's the bottom line: If you want to cause your real estate business to explode the way mine did, then from now on, Instagram is going to be your main portal to engage and build relationships with people. I'm not asking you to throw out everything else and just focus on Instagram. But in this day and age, it would be a huge mistake for you to think that your real estate business survives on those other things. They are no longer the "main way" that people do business now, so don't plan your business's success around them. Optimize your results on those other tools by ensuring that you're using social media in general (and in my opinion, Instagram specifically) to drive the majority of your leads and sales.

If I've been able to change your mindset on the role of Instagram in your real estate business, I've done my job with this chapter. Now, let's start talking about the key ways you can begin building your audience and your brand there.

4. DEVELOPING YOUR PILLARS OF CONTENT

IN THE WORLD of social media, building a loyal following takes more than just making a few posts, following a bunch of people, liking a few posts, etc. You can always tell the people who are using social media casually because that's exactly what they do. And that's fine if that's all you want from it. But if you are going to turn your social media into a major marketing tool to make your real estate business explode, it's going to take a lot more than "dabbling." You have to be purposeful in your approach. Most importantly--if you're going to convince people to follow you online, you have to give them a *reason* to do it.

That's where your content strategy comes in. I refer to this as your "Pillars of Content."

Developing and posting excellent content is the foundation for your success on social media. Good content keeps people interested and engaged while establishing you as an authority in your field. As we'll see, posting consistently also gets you in front of more people more often. In this chapter, we're going to talk about how posting good content regularly will help build your brand as an agent and attract clients who are looking for someone like you. We'll also dig into what exactly makes good content and how to develop a winning content strategy. And again, while these principles will serve well on all social media platforms, we're going to keep our conversation focused mainly on Instagram since it's the cornerstone of our specific approach.

Before we talk about the Pillars of Content and how they work for you, let's lay a foundation for those pillars by talking about the importance of content in general and how you should structure your profile to support that content.

Why Content Is King

When thinking about creating content for Instagram or any other platform, there are two key ingredients to success: 1) Posting quality content; and 2) posting consistently. The key to taking ownership of this principle is to understand how and why the principle works. So let's talk for a minute about WHY it's so critical that you post quality, consistent content, and HOW posting good content gets you a bigger following and more leads. There are essentially two reasons why content matters:

1) The more frequently you post, the more your posts are seen.

This is due to the way Instagram indexes user posts. There are simply too many people on social media for every one of our followers to see everything we post all the time. So instead of trying to show everyone everything, Instagram's algorithm "feeds" us posts based what it thinks we want to see based on our prior use. (That's why they call it a "feed.") When someone is posting content often--and when it's *good* content that evokes likes and comments--Instagram assumes their followers want to see more of that content, and so your posts show up more frequently in their feeds.

There's more. Instagram also prioritizes content that gets a lot of engagement. When certain posts evoke a significant number of likes and comments, Instagram believes those posts are relevant and "popular," so it will share them on more of your followers' feeds.

Why is that?

Simple: Instagram is designed so that consistent, relevant content gets seen by more people. When you post good content regularly, you expand your reach.

Maybe you've noticed this on your own feed. You may be following thousands of people, but it seems like 20 people show up more often in your feed than everyone else. That's because those 20 people are posting more frequently, and chances are they're posting about stuff that interests you. That's precisely how Instagram works.

Now...to make this work to your advantage, your goal is to *become* one of those top 20 people on your followers' feeds. The key to accomplishing that is to post consistently. Tons of content. Interesting content.

2) Posting quality content builds loyalty from your followers.

The previous point was all about convincing the Instagram algorithm that you've got content worth sharing. This point is about actually creating *good* content that humans want to see and engage with. What does quality content look like? We'll go more in-depth on this question momentarily, but for now, quality content is content that generates interest, educates, informs, or evokes a response. You want people to hit the "like" button. You want them to comment. Not just to get Instagram to share it more, but because when people engage with your content, they tend to remember you. That's your goal: to build awareness and mindshare with your followers.

So if you're a real estate broker, and you're posting interesting content that people appreciate and engage with...when those people are ready to buy or sell a home, who are they going to think of first?

That guy on that billboard they saw one time?

That gal who sent them the postcard in the mail?

Maybe in an earlier time. Today, probably not so much.

You know who they WILL think of? That interesting guy or gal they follow on Instagram who does those cool posts and who happens to sell real estate. That broker who keeps showing up in their feed.

See the potential here?

Posting for Two Audiences

To boil down everything we've said so far and make it easy for you to remember, think of it this way. By creating quality, consistent content, you're basically posting for two audiences:

1. You're posting for Instagram's algorithm; and
2. You're posting for humans.

It's very important to keep both of these in mind when creating content because if you only focus on one or the other, your content won't be as effective. If you post all the time trying to get Instagram to show more of your stuff, but your content is lousy (for example, trivial crap no one's interested in or bad photos no one wants to see), you may show up in more people's feeds for a while, but no one's going to engage you-- and if the content is annoying, they'll just unfollow you. On the other hand, if you post great content for humans, but you never post enough (or share content consistently), fewer people will see the content, and the algorithm may think your posts aren't top-quality because they don't get much engagement. To build your brand and generate loyalty from your followers, you need to play to *both* audiences: Instagram and humans.

Optimizing Your Instagram Profile

One key ingredient to a successful content strategy--and one that many real estate brokers and other professionals overlook--is having an Instagram profile that speaks well of you and your business. Yes, most of your followers are going to see your posts on their feed rather than by going to your profile--but first, they have to follow you! And to follow you, they need to visit your profile.

In terms of content, your profile is the first bit of content your future followers are going to see. It's your one chance to make a first impression. What people see on your profile, even subtle things about it, can affect whether they click the "Follow" button. Even if they went to your profile intending follow you, if they see something that turns them off on your profile, they could change their mind. So optimizing your Instagram profile should be your first step in building a quality content plan.

Specifically, I recommend focusing your attention on the following aspects of your profile...

- *Your profile picture.* This is the first thing people notice when they come to your profile, so make it count. Some people use a photo of themselves, either a headshot or a candid shot; others might use their company logo. I highly recommend using a high-quality photograph of yourself, professionally taken, instead of a logo. People want to follow a person, not a company--and when we start getting into the Pillars of Content themselves, you'll understand why it's important to have a personal feel to your profile.

- *Your bio.* You have a lot of leeway as to how to make your bio stand out--just not a lot of space. So put some thought into how you want to present yourself here. You want to be seen as a professional, but also someone interesting, someone with a story to tell. You might want to include some sort of call to action with a URL. For me, I've chosen the short-and-sweet, straightforward approach. I list my relevant credentials (leader of a team for my brokerage, founder of Very Social, etc.), and a Linktree link, which is basically a portal to a list of links like my website, my listings, other social media accounts, etc., where people can learn more about me.

- *Instagram Story Highlights.* I'll explain the reason for this shortly, but for now, just know you should be posting Instagram Stories frequently as part of your content strategy. When your Stories expire, Instagram lets you save them as Highlights, which you can group by category. If you look on my Instagram page, you'll see I've got a bunch of categories for my Highlights, including listings, tours, events, travel, behind-the-scenes, events, and so on.

- *Your Grid.* Here's where some important planning comes in, because with Instagram, you don't want to focus just on individual posts, pictures, and videos--you want to think about how these posts look when they appear together in the grid format. Instagram builds this grid in order from newest to oldest posts, and you can't switch the order. When you make Instagram your main portal, people are going to be visiting your Instagram profile before even going to your website--so the grid is what people will look at when they first type your name in the search bar and pull up your profile. You want the look of your grid to be a good representation of you, so the posts need to be aligned and arranged to have a good aesthetic together. The pictures should have the same sort of filter or look and feel so it's apparent that they belong together. The way you arrange your grid thus becomes part of your branding, your watermark. For clients of my social media company, Very Social, we plan these grids out very strategically a month in advance so every addition to the grid makes sense visually.

What Are Your Pillars of Content?

Now that we've covered these basics, let's dive into the Pillars of Content themselves--what they are, how to use them, and why they work.

As we've alluded to before, successful social media branding is not just posting about your business. It's much more holistic, more human. More *social*. As a real estate broker on social media, you're essentially marketing and branding yourself. And that makes sense because your product isn't actually real estate. The product you're marketing isn't your specific listings. Your product is you. *You are your brand.*

But you're also a *person*--and a person is more than just one thing. I'm not just a real estate broker, and I'm not just all about selling homes. I'm also a husband and a dad. I'm an entrepreneur. I'm a social media enthusiast. I love New York City. I love good food. These interests of mine, these parts of who I am--they all inform my own Pillars of Content. I take these various parts of my life, my passions, and my personality, and from them I have created a set of categories that I post about regularly on social media.

So for you, your Pillars of Content will be different than

mine. Yes, as a fellow real estate agent, you'll have at least one pillar in common with me. *Real estate* is your first pillar, and it's a big one. (Your second pillar should be *community expert*, and I'll get to that in a minute.) But you'll choose other pillars based on your interests and your lifestyle. Are you a parent? Are you a golfer? Do you like books and movies? Are you a foodie? A photographer? What are your hobbies? What causes do you care about? Make a list of these things, and then narrow the list down to a few things that are most important to you. These become your Pillars of Content--the categories of content that you'll post about on a regular basis.

Once you have identified your Pillars of Content, you'll develop subsets or sub-pillars based on those categories. Using myself as an example--for the real estate pillar, I have subsets that include success stories, market updates, property show-ings, video tours, expert advice, etc. Under the "dad" pillar, there are goofy pictures and videos of me with my kid, photos of the family at breakfast, and so on.

Now, granted, a lot of this is stuff you might post normally on a personal profile. But by grouping it all within your Pillars of Content, you're basically organizing it--giving it a sense of structure so you can post purposefully rather than randomly.

Benefits of Using the Pillars of Content Approach

Hopefully, as I describe this approach to planning and orga-nizing your Instagram content, the wheels are turning in your mind, and you're seeing the potential here. But just in case you're uncertain, let me talk about why this approach to content strategy works so well:

It destroys social media "writers' block."

Most real estate brokers and other professionals agree with me when I say you can't just post about real estate. But the inevitable next question is, "What else do I post about?" One of the biggest reasons people fail at social media isn't that they don't *want* to post--they just don't know *what* to post. Setting up the Pillars of Content helps you see just how much great stuff you have to share on social media, and it gives you a structure for planning how and when to post it. When you master this concept, you'll never be left wondering what you have to talk about. Writer's block becomes a thing of the past.

It generates multiple connection points with your followers.

Remember, almost everyone on social media is a potential customer because almost everyone will be in the market to buy or sell a home at some point. But most of your followers won't be in the market *right this minute*, and you don't want them only paying attention to you when they're specifically thinking about real estate. Having multiple pillars helps you connect with people on a wider range of interests for the long term. For example, if you are a fan of fishing and you post once in a while about your latest catch or your favorite lake, you might gain followers and start engaging with other fishing enthusiasts. If one of those people decides to buy a lakefront home in your area, and they remember you're an angler but you *also* sell real estate...BAM. You've just landed a hot lead that you probably never would have gotten if all you did was post about your listings.

It's Okay to Have Some Overlap

When I say "Pillars of Content," I'm talking about a structure and framework for you to organize your postings. But that doesn't mean every post of yours has to stay in its own lane under its own pillar. It's okay to have overlap between them. So if one day I take my kid out to Central Park, I might post about that (the "dad pillar"), but it's totally okay once in a while if I work in a sentence about my favorite neighborhoods around Central Park (the "real estate pillar"). It's also fine if I mention that a new listing I put up just happens to be next door to my favorite restaurant (the "food pillar"). Basically, with this method, you're putting *real* stuff in with your *real estate* stuff. And the same goes for all the other pillars that you have chosen--all of these categories intermingle because they are all part of who you are as a person and what is important to you. That's part of making your social media presence look and feel more authentic.

Building Mindshare with Your Social Media Audience

Being "top-of-mind" is a term thrown around quite often in marketing circles. It basically refers to keeping your name and brand in front of people regularly in the hope that you'll be "top-of-mind" when they need what you're selling. But in social media-land, that concept tends to ring shallow because it's a throwback to mass advertising. One of the biggest reasons why you need multiple Pillars of Content is that if you use your social media to post *only* about real estate, you're basically using social media as a mass marketing tool.

And that's the fastest way to get ignored.

This is a common snare that many real estate agents fall into--and it's one of the main reasons why so many of them think social media doesn't work. They mistakenly think that the way to stay "top-of-mind" with their followers is to post constantly about real estate so their name is associated indelibly with their profession. The problem is that people are smarter than that. That approach to social media is a form of manipulation, and people don't like to be manipulated.

So instead of worrying about being "top-of-mind," I want to encourage you to explore a deeper type of connection with your audience: building *mindshare* with your followers.[1]

The term *mindshare* is used to describe the amount of attention that a person or idea has in the public consciousness. It's similar to *market share* except that while *market share* refers to the percentage of total consumers who buy into a certain brand, *mindshare* refers to the amount of brain space your brand occupies with your audience. And it's more than just *how often* they think of you--it's how they *feel* about you when you come to mind.

Your audience inhabits a world that's constantly changing. The difference between great and mediocre marketing on social media is the difference between being heard in this space and being ignored. Mindshare isn't a goal; it's a byproduct of saying something worth thinking about.

You need to remember that most of your followers on Instagram and other platforms aren't real estate agents. They don't live and breathe this stuff like we do, and frankly, most of them could care less when you close on a million-dollar property--that is, UNLESS you've built a connection with them, a rapport that's based on other interests. That's why you need multiple Pillars of Content, not just real estate. It's these *other things* you'll post about that build mindshare so that when you do post the occasional "Hey, I just closed a huge sale!", they're more likely to give a crap about it and even celebrate it with you.

I don't know about you, but I read social media posts, it's the ones that tell a story and spark conversations that keep me engaged. So that's what I try to emulate with my own posts. When we create content to share knowledge instead of just pushing out real estate information all day long, then we make connections with people that are stronger and last longer than if we just play the top-of-mind game.

So as you work on developing mindshare with your social media audience, try to get into their minds. Think about what matters to them, not just you. Then ask yourself: *What can I say to them that's worth thinking about?* Then with that in mind, use your posts to let your followers know, in a human voice, what you think and why you think it. Be *human*, and build a human connection. That's the best way to build mindshare on social media.

How to Create Content that Generates Leads

By this point, I no longer need to convince you of the importance of putting up lots of content on Instagram and other social media, and the Pillars of Content approach helps give you a framework for doing so. But content for content's sake isn't necessarily going to get you results. If you post a bunch of content that isn't helpful or engaging, it might actually end up being a bit off-putting and annoying, and you might even lose some followers. So the next piece of this puzzle is to learn how to create *compelling* content.

Remember why you're doing this. As a real estate agent, your goal with social media isn't just to gain a following; you hope that at least *some* of these followers will eventually become clients. If they don't, you will have wasted your time. So let's go over some tips for developing content that is more likely to keep your audience interested and eventually convert to more leads.

Become the local expert on your community.

Remember earlier when I said your second Pillar of Content should be *community expert*? Think of yourself as the unofficial mayor of your city or town--the cheerleader on social media for all the reasons your town is a great place to live. You need to know the history of the area. You need to know the different neighborhoods and what's great about them. You need to know what's going on in the community, the latest events and happenings. Learn about it all--and post about it. Be genuinely excited and enthusiastic about your community. Also, you need to be keeping tabs on what the new businesses are, what the hottest restaurant is, and then you need to be connecting with these places by tagging them, by re-posting them, by giving them a shout-out. Creating content about your community builds trust with your audience that you know what you're talking about, and if they ever find themselves in a position where they're going to buy or sell real estate, they'll believe you're the guy or gal with the inside scoop.

Utilize Instagram Stories and Highlights.

I've mentioned these features a few times before, but there are five great reasons why I feel they're especially useful for real estate brokers:

1. *Stories are highly popular.* A lot of users pay more attention to Instagram Stories than they do to their feeds.

Stories give a sense of immediacy. Since Instagram Stories disappear in 24 hours, it creates a sense that people need to pay attention NOW.

1. *Stories are the best way on Instagram to share other people's content.* Sharing awesome, fun or inspiring content that others have posted is a great way to connect on any social media platform. On Instagram, you do that with Stories. For any post in your feed that you want to share, simply tap the airplane-looking icon and select "add post to your story."
2. *Stories invite deeper engagement.* People can't just hit the "like" button with Stories, and if they want to comment, they have to do so via direct message

(DM). I find this encourages followers to start direct conversations with me, and followers who are interested enough to chat are more likely to become leads.

3. *Stories give you a way to categorize content.* By converting Stories to Instagram Highlights when they expire, you can create a whole subset of interesting categories so people visiting your profile can click to view Stories that cover specific topics they're interested in.

If you remember, the $3 million sale that started me on this social media journey began with a follower sending me a DM in response to an Instagram Story. I believe in Stories. They promote engagement, and engagement creates leads. Learn how to use Stories, and post a lot of them.

Educate and inform your audience.

This usually falls squarely within the *real estate* pillar. As the local authority on real estate, make it your mission to educate your followers on what they need to know to find their dream home, how to get the best price when selling a home, what they need to know about the current state of the market, etc. You can do this with sporadic helpful tips in your posts, or you might even utilize Instagram Live to do a free webinar once in a while. Again, this sets you up as the expert people will think of first when it's time to buy or sell a piece of property.

Use only high-quality images and text.

Avoid blurry, grainy, low-resolution photos. If you can't get high-resolution photos from your smartphone, get a better smartphone, or better yet, invest in a DSLR camera. When you write a post, make sure it's compelling, well-written, and typo-free. If you're not great with the written word, it's worth a few extra dollars to hire a copywriter or proofreader to go over your posts before they go live. These may seem like subtle things, but they go a long way toward making you appear like a professional--someone people can trust if they decide to do business with you. Remember, your posts are part of your branding.

Post content that encourages engagement.

We'll talk about the importance of engagement in a future chapter, but for now, just know that a key part of Instagram's algorithm is that it prioritizes posts that generate engagement. In other words, when people like and comment on your post, Instagram sees it as as a post other people might want to see and engage with, so it starts showing it to more people. By the same token, if a lot of your posts generate likes and comments, Instagram will give your posts more priority in general, and you're more likely to show up at or near the top of people's feeds.

One easy way to promote engagement is to ask questions in some of your posts. So for example, here in NYC, I might post a photo of my favorite restaurant on the Upper West Side and ask if any of my followers have been there--or maybe I'll ask for recommendations on what Broadway show to see, or ask what their favorite ice cream place is here in town. One cool thing we often do is post an Instagram Story comparing two things (for example, two remodeled kitchens) and put a button on the Story that they can click to vote for their favorite. You can be creative here as long as it gets people to respond.

Keys to Developing Strong Graphics

I want to go back to the point of high-quality images for a moment. Remember, as a photo-based platform, Instagram is primarily a visual medium. Not everyone on Instagram posts the highest-quality stuff, but if you're a real estate agent on Instagram, there's an expectation that your visuals should be above average. Now, I'm not saying you need to be a photographer (I'm not), but really examine your graphics and ask yourself if they are truly helping or hurting your marketing.

For real estate agents, having professional standards with photography is nothing new. Most of us agents hire professional photographers to photograph our listings (and if you don't, you should). What I'm saying is you need to carry that same standard of professionalism over to Instagram--because doing so sends a message to your followers that YOU are a professional. Let's go over a couple of ways you can develop a strong visual body of content.

Hire a professional photographer.

Yes, you read that right. You need to have your Instagram photos done professionally--or at least, a significant portion of them. I'm not saying you can't take a few photos yourself with a good smartphone, but don't post them unless they're truly stellar. For the rest, the more professional the photos look, the better.

Now, if you're balking at the cost of this, let me say there are creative ways to minimize the costs. For me, one trick I like to do is hire a photographer once a quarter for a few hours, pick two or three locations and a few wardrobe changes, and just get as many different photos as I can. Then I can take that content and schedule it out over the next three months. It keeps my content diverse while keeping my costs down, sometimes averaging less than a dollar a post.

Create a consistent look for your graphics and photos.

Instagram offers plenty of photo-editing and graphics options on-board, including filters, Instagram Type Mode (which lets you overlay text on your stories) and more. But if you don't want to look like every Instagrammer out there, you'll have to evolve past the basic onboard tools. To *really* stand out, I recommend that you come up with a consistent palette of filters, fonts, color schemes and graphics that you use on all your content. This way, you're effectively creating a visual brand. Your goal is for followers to recognize your posts before they see your username on them. To do this right, you're going to want to hire a graphic designer to develop this palette for you.

Again, let's talk about cost--because hiring a graphic designer is indeed an investment. But if you were focusing on the conventional marketing methods (i.e., billboards, mailers, TV ads, etc., you'd need a graphic designer for those, as well. If social media is now your main marketing tool, and Instagram is your main portal, why not invest in making it look as professional as possible?

Creating a Posting Schedule

We've talked about setting up Pillars of Content to give you some structure and inspiration for creating lots of content. We've also talked about some ways to make that content stand out. Now, let's tie it all together. Once you have these pieces in place, what does a good content strategy actually look like?

I've said it before: One of the keys to being visible on Instagram and other social media outlets is to post consistently. By "consistently," I also mean often.

How often? My recommendation is to post at least once a day on your social media platforms--more if you can swing it.

Any less than that, and you won't be keeping yourself in front of your followers enough to be remembered.

But this presents a couple of new challenges. How do you create THAT MUCH content so you can post that often? And how do you keep THAT MUCH content from turning your grid into a cluttered mess?

The answer to both questions: *Plan ahead.* Develop a posting schedule.

Look, I get it. If you were to create original posts on all your social media in real-time daily, or twice daily, or 4-5 times daily, that's all you'd be doing. When you start getting leads, you won't have time to show them homes because social media will be your full-time gig. So instead, use the strategies I've given you above, create a bunch of content with them, and then schedule it all out. One of the easiest ways to do this yourself is to use a scheduling tool like Hootsuite, SocialPilot, Buffer, Sendible, or any of a host of others. For my Very Social clients, my team plans posts a month in advance.

There are two huge advantages to scheduling your content:

1. *It frees up your time.* It's much better to devote a block of time to creating and planning a bunch of posts than trying to do everything "on the fly" and thinking every day about what you should post that day. Once you've set up your schedule, you can put it to the side and focus on other things. It also gives you more time during the day to engage people more directly on Instagram, which we'll cover in another chapter.

2. *It helps you create a consistent look and feel.* Planning ahead helps you stagger and alternate posts from various pillars so you don't get clusters of posts about just one topic. For example, you post about your latest sale, then do a post about your kid's soccer game, then a post about your favorite

restaurant in town, then a post about current market trends, then ask your followers to comment on what their favorite summer drink is. Planning helps you keep the content fresh. In addition, planning helps you maintain a pleasing look to your grid so everything looks like it belongs in the right place.

Now, I'm not saying you can't post on the fly once in a while. (After all, that's the "Insta" part of "Instagram," right?) You can certainly weigh in on a huge breaking news story (especially in real estate), or grab a picture of an amazing sunset while you're out with your family and post it right then ("Hey, are you guys seeing this?"). But scheduling your posts keeps a lot of the heavy lifting away from your daily schedule so you'll always have content showing up even when you don't have the time or mental energy to figure something out on the fly.

We've covered a lot of ground in this chapter, but the main takeaway is this: Instagram is more than just another outlet for posting photos. It's a powerful tool that can help you build your brand as a real estate agent, especially if it's used correctly. The key to making it work is *content*--developing quality content and posting it strategically. There are other pieces we'll be covering in future chapters, but if you can get the content piece down, you're already more than halfway to turning your social media into a lead-generating machine.

5. USING VIDEO TO ELEVATE YOUR BRAND

NOW THAT WE'VE covered the content piece in general, let's expand the conversation from Instagram to talk about one type of content that can be exceptionally powerful for you as a real estate broker: the use of video to build your brand.

When most people think about video these days, they immediately think of YouTube, and with good reason. As I write this, YouTube actually has more users than Instagram--in fact, with nearly 2.3 billion users, it's second only to Facebook in number of accounts. YouTube has produced thousands of budding Internet stars, launched music careers and acting careers, all by providing a platform for people to post videos of themselves and build a fan base of millions.

But YouTube is not the only social media platform where video lives. And I'm not just talking about TikTok (although we will cover TikTok). In fact, virtually every social media platform now offers some functionality for recording, editing and posting video, as well as sharing video from other sites. Instagram itself has evolved from strictly photos to enable video in several capacities. Not only can you record and post videos up to 60 seconds directly on your profile, you can also record longer-form videos on IGTV and post a short clip on the feed to entice people to click through. You can also integrate video into Stories, and more recently, Instagram Reels enables a suite of fun effects to produce short-form videos similar to TikTok.

Now, I'm not saying that you need to become the latest YouTube sensation--because you don't. But real estate marketing is visual, and video tends to engage today's social media audience even more effectively than still photos. So the strategic, effective use of video can elevate your social media marketing game to a whole new level. And just like social media itself, if you're ignoring this powerful tool, you could be leaving money on the table.

How I Utilize Video in Social Media

The fact is, I could write a whole other book on the various ways real estate brokers can use video to maximize their sales--and maybe one day I will. But for the sake of time and space, I think rather than tell you how YOU should use it, I'll just talk about what I do--how I have come to integrate video into my marketing strategy--so you can see the potential of it and draw from my example to come up with your own plan.

Video Listings

As I mentioned earlier when telling my story, I discovered the potential of video marketing when I owned the puppy store in Florida. I posted videos on my website of me playing with the puppies--and there's nothing like seeing a video like that to make people want a puppy of their own. When I became a real estate agent, I realized early on that video could be a highly effective tool in selling real estate, especially with high-end properties (which NYC has a *lot* of).

Some NYC agents who specialize in luxury apartments go all out, buying TV time and producing their own shows that highlight their latest listings. But as you can imagine, that takes a huge outlay of cash, and most agents can only afford to run those shows on Sunday mornings when most people aren't watching. I felt I could do better by utilizing social media. So I started by creating video listings of some of my properties, posting them on YouTube, and sharing them on my other social media platforms or in my newsletters to try and drive traffic to them. I wouldn't just do panning shots of the apartment; I'd take one or two of my teammates to banter with, and we'd shoot video in the apartment with us talking about the features of the unit, showing the views from the deck, talking about the neighborhood, and basically taking viewers on a tour of the place. We'd make these videos light, upbeat, and enthusiastic, and viewers loved them not just because they were fun, but because they painted a clearer picture of what the home really looked like.

It turned out to be a highly effective strategy. Utilizing YouTube and other social media platforms, we were able to put these video listings directly in front of thousands of potential buyers online. Today, video listings are part of the Unique Selling Proposition for the Garson Team--one of the things we're known for. Because they work.

Expanding My Use of Video

I'm a big believer in the idea that "if it's working, do more of it." As my use of social media evolved, so did the integration of videos, and as my team and I got better at making our videos, we started using them for other purposes. People seemed to enjoy seeing me talk on the video listings as much as they liked the properties themselves--so we sort of leaned into that, and I started posting more videos around my other Pillars of Content. I started exploring Instagram's video features more, as well as platforms like Facebook and TikTok.

Today, my use of video as part of my social media presence

is broad and diverse. I expanded from video listings to other topics. I do videos about food, about fashion, about being a Dad (including goofy moments with my kid). One time I did a video called "Day in the Life of an Entrepreneur" and took viewers through my whole day in about 8 minutes. Sometimes, I just shoot videos with my iPhone. Sometimes, I use professional videographers. For special projects, I may hire a high-end videographer who brings a sound and camera crew and lots of expensive gear. Then I have another person who's more of a casual videographer. It just depends on what I'm trying to film and why.

Some of you may once again be choking on the potential costs for doing these videos...so once again, let me set your mind at ease. The key is to re-edit and repurpose your videos for multiple platforms. This social media world is so diverse that there are plenty of ways to cut and recut the same content so it comes off as fresh on all platforms. So when I create a video, I ask the videographer/editor to create multiple versions out of multiple clips. So there will be one version (typically the full version) for YouTube, and we'll cut another short clip for IGTV, another for Facebook. Then maybe we'll do a juiced-up clip with text and filters on it for Instagram Reels, and another for TikTok. And maybe we'll stagger the videos so they don't all post at the same time, or even the same week. I can create all this content from the same video session, so the cost gets spread out--and that's what makes it affordable. I have a different audience for each platform, so I create unique content for that audience. I don't feel comfortable now posting the same video on five different platforms. I like cutting it up and creating different versions of the video for each platform.

Don't Be Camera Shy

Another thing I think a lot of agents struggle with is the idea that "nobody wants to see me on video." What they're really saying is that they don't want to see *themselves* on video. A lot of people feel the same way about photos--they don't like posting pictures of themselves.

But that's not what your followers think. They *want* to see photos and videos of you.

I get it. It can make you feel very self-conscious to see yourself on camera, especially video--especially the first few times you do it. "Do I really look that way when I talk?" "Do I really do that with my hands?" "I look mad."

Granted, every personality is different, and you don't have to be like me or do it exactly like me to make it work for you. But to get the best results from social media marketing, I want to encourage you to push through and get over the idea of being camera shy.

It's okay to take baby steps. It's okay to start out by maybe doing some video tours of listings while you're behind the camera narrating--or to do a webinar with just your voice over a slideshow. It's okay to practice with video for a time before making one public. But at some point, you need to make the leap. The videos don't have to be perfect, and you don't have to be perfect. (You should see some of MY early videos.) But the more you do it, the better you'll get--and you'll make a better connection with your followers in the process. They want a face and a voice to go with the name. And when they decide it's time to buy or sell a home, you want it to be your name, face, and voice they think of.

Your Own Reality Show

Perhaps you've caught on by now that the people who find the most success on social media are those who treat it in some ways like a broadcast, and their followers are their fan base. When you add video to the mix, it can feel even more like that. In a sense, you're hosting your own reality show, giving your followers a window into your life, your business, and the stuff you care about. Like anything else, it takes practice to make it good--but if you'll take it seriously and hone your social media chops, you'll learn how to make compelling content. And before long, your followers will be hooked. They will pay attention when your posts show up in their feed. They will HAVE to know what comes next.

And that's exactly where you want them.

6. EXPANDING YOUR AUDIENCE--
AND YOUR INFLUENCE

ANYONE REMEMBER *FIELD OF DREAMS*? It's that Oscar-winning film from the late 1980s where Kevin Costner plays an Iowa farmer who hears voices telling him to build a baseball diamond in the middle of a cornfield where dead baseball legends come to play. It's a heartwarming film that produced one of the most memorable lines in film history: "If you build it, he will come."

We often carry that mindset into the projects we take on. "If we build it, they will come."

If we start an event, people will show up for it.

If we build a website, people will visit it.

If we start posting content on social media, people will follow us.

"If we build it, they will come."

Except it's not true.

That idea works in *Field of Dreams*, but not in real life.

People won't show up to a party just because you have one. You won't have millions of visitors to your website just because it looks snazzy. And you won't get tens of thousands of Instagram followers just by posting content.

Why not? Because in the real world, people aren't like the

ghosts in *Field of Dreams*. They don't just cosmically "know" when something is being "built" for them. *They have to be told about it.*

They have to be invited to the party. They have to know your website exists. They have to know who you are on social media before they follow you.

You can have the best-looking Instagram profile of any real estate agent you know. You can put up the best photos, the best videos, post the most compelling content, and still your social media presence could basically go nowhere. Oh, you'll get a few followers here and there if you post consistently, just because of Instagram's algorithm. But for the most part, you're just sitting there.

Why?

Don't misunderstand. You need the content. You need a social media presence. You need to have a place for people to come to. But simply building it isn't enough. *You need something more.*

So here we come to the next piece of the puzzle--the next key that you need to turn your social media presence into a marketing machine.

I'm talking about *engagement.*

You have to engage people online.

Social media is, well, *social.* In the social media space, engagement is how you let people know you're there. Engagement is how people find out about you and the great party you're hosting on your profile.

Here's how engagement works. When you "like" other people's posts, they come around and "like" yours. When you follow them, they follow you back. When you comment on their posts, they're more likely to comment on yours. When you message them directly, they're likely to reply.

And it works both ways. When someone comments on your post, answer them. Then find a post of theirs that you like and comment on it. When someone reaches out via DM, reply to them.

Be social. On social media. (Novel concept, I know.)

Let's go back to the metaphor of using social media to make your real estate business "explode." If a good social media profile and good content are the fuel, engagement is the match that lights it.

I know we just talked in the last chapter about your social media being like a broadcast or reality show. But it's actually a bit more textured than that. If it were just a "broadcast," you would talk, and people would listen. But in social media, people get to talk back in the comments, and you get the chance to reply. It's more than a broadcast--it's a *conversation.* Or at least, that's what you want it to be. That's why engagement needs to be a key part of your social media strategy. The more you engage, the more of a following you'll get, and the more rapport and trust you'll build within that following.

It's a Time Commitment

Now, here's the part you probably don't want to hear. There really are no shortcuts when it comes to engagement. Unlike your content, you can't automate it, you can't schedule it, and you can't let it run in the background.

There's no getting around it. *Engagement takes time.* Doing it right means taking hours out of your day. Every day.

Do you know why I'm so big on planning your content and scheduling it out? Because we all only have so many hours in the day. You should be budgeting a certain amount of time each day for social media, and if you spend all that time figuring out what to post, you won't have enough time to engage people. There are ways to save time with content creation. Engagement is more organic, and it takes the time that it takes. You can't cut corners with it. So by planning and scheduling your content, you free up more time to engage, comment, and dialogue--to actually be *social* with your following.

The Snowball Effect

Here's the good news about engagement: The more you do it, the more effective it becomes. The results start snowballing. It's like a feedback loop--the more you engage, the greater your results are, and the greater your results are, the more people want to engage with you.

It goes something like this: You invest the time needed to engage--leaving likes and comments, sharing posts, and so on. People notice that you're engaging and reach out to engage back. Then you respond to those comments and start a conversation. So you have more and better interactions which lead to a higher-quality, more engaged following overall.

Now, here's where things get really fun--and here's why I told you to ramp up your content. When Instagram detects you're posting consistently, it starts putting your content in front of more people. But when more people start *engaging* with that content, Instagram likes it even more. Your visibility kicks into a higher gear, and your stuff gets seen even more often by more people. You get more followers, you follow them back. You keep interacting with them, they keep interacting with you. Then these people start sharing your content with their friends. Before long, you're seeing 10 new followers a day. Then 30 a day. Then 100 a day.

It's exponential growth.

It's not too much longer before your following starts to outrun you. It starts growing faster than you can keep up with it.

It's kind of a paradox. Your goal with engagement is to get so many followers that you couldn't possibly respond to all of them. And that tipping point can happen fast if you're diligent about it.

Another way to look at it is the principle of gravity. Did you ever learn in science class that you'd weigh more on Jupiter than you do on Earth? (2.4 times as much, to be precise.) The reason is that the more mass an object has, the greater force of gravity it exerts. Jupiter has more mass than Earth, so it attracts other objects with more force. Likewise, a black hole is so dense that its gravity is inescapable, and it starts pulling everything into it with an incredible amount of force.

At some point when you're growing your following, your social media presence starts exerting its own gravity. Your following starts growing almost without your help simply because you've become so visible online that people who are interested in what you're talking about can easily find and follow you on their own. And the bigger your following gets, the faster your following grows.

My Own Results

Once I got hold of the power of using social media to grow my real estate business, I started pouring huge amounts of time into creating content and engaging people. I crunched the numbers after a year, and here's what I saw:

- My number of Instagram followers increased by nearly 200 percent. (In other words--they tripled.)
- My number of likes per post increased by 125 percent.
- Comments on my posts increased by 250 percent. (In other words, people were more likely to take time to write a comment than just to hit the "like" button.)
- Responses to my Instagram stories went up by 150 percent.

Oh, I almost forgot. You might be wondering how all this social media activity translated to actual sales.

How about $100 million in real estate transactions?

How about $1 million in commissions?

Yes, I spent some money. I invested in quality content. But between what I spent and what I made...my return on investment (ROI) was *1200 percent.*

Are you convinced yet?

More Followers Means More Influence

Not only does a larger following mean you have more eyeballs on your posts, it means you have more influence. *Influence* means you're viewed with a greater measure of authority than the average person on social media. When someone has thousands of followers and gets hundreds or even thousands of likes on their posts, people tend to pay more attention to what that person is saying. So if you're a real estate agent with a huge following and tons of engagement on your posts, what you say will ring with more authority than someone who has, say, 100 followers and almost no engagement. This is especially true when you talk about something within your field of expertise (in this case, real estate).

So let's tie this back in with leveraging social media to get more leads and generate more sales. Being active and visible on social media naturally means you'll have more mindshare with your followers when they decide it's time to look for a new home or sell an existing one. But what if they are following several real estate agents in their local area? They are only going to pick one of you. Whom are they most likely to choose?

You got it. The one with the most perceived authority. *The one with greater influence.* Why? Because in their minds, the one with more authority also has more expertise and is more likely to get the job done for them.

Practical Methods for Engagement to Get More
Followers--and More Influence

So now that you understand the power of engagement on
social media, let's talk about how to do it most effectively. The
obvious things to do are to follow people, like and comment
on other people's posts, reply back when someone comments
on your stuff--we've covered that ground. But there are other
strategies you can implement that will maximize your efforts
and focus your energy toward growing the kind of following
you want to have. So let's go over some of these now.

**Search for others to follow who share your expertise and
interests.**

Use the Instagram search feature to find other people in
your same field (real estate) as well as those who share other
interests among your Pillars of Content. Try doing searches
using specific keywords and hashtags. For example, if I were
looking for other real estate agents in NYC, I'd do searches on
"New York City real estate" or "Greenwich Village real estate"
or hashtags #NYCrealestate or #upperwestside. If you're a
foodie, do the same with food interests. If you're interested in
golf, search for golf enthusiasts. Find people who have a good
following and good engagement, follow them, like and
comment on their posts. Then look at who is following *those*
people, follow them and comment. Try sending DMs to a few
of them. Chances are some of these people are going to check
you out, follow you back, comment on your stuff, etc. This
method is a great way to strategically connect with people who
are likely to start and maintain conversations with you. Not
just any followers--followers who are truly interested in what
you're saying.

Now, I can almost see the wheels turning in some of your
minds. *Did he just say to follow other real estate agents?*

Yep.

Aren't they the competition?

Maybe. Not always.

But really? Follow them?

YES.

Here's why. You're looking for people who might eventually buy from you--but you're not ONLY looking for those people. You're also looking to network. The real estate industry is competitive, but it's also highly collaborative. By following other agents, you're building relationships within your industry. They don't all have to be agents in your town--they can be anywhere. And some of them will have different areas of expertise than you--for instance, you might be focused on single-family starter homes while someone else's expertise is in luxury condos. The point is--connect with them. They won't buy from you, but they MIGHT refer you to some people. And that's still gold.

Find and follow other businesses in your community.

Another great way to get relevant followers is to network with other business owners. Again, think of yourself as the unofficial mayor of your town, or even the president of the local Chamber of Commerce. Business owners are your allies. Retail shops, restaurants, spas, bars, gyms...you get the idea. Not only does connecting with these people help you become an authority on where people in your town can go for a great cocktail or haircut, it also becomes your virtual business networking community--a place where you can give each other referrals.

Do shoutouts.

Tying in with the previous point, when you make friends with other businesses or community leaders online, make a point of mentioning them in your posts--and put their username into the post. "Hey, guys, I just went by @mikesfishandchips and got the best fried shrimp EVER." And maybe you post it with a photo taken with your smartphone of you and "Mike" from @mikesfishandchips. This is an excellent form of engagement because it provides an instant link to that other person's profile and gives people a chance to follow them. And when you do a good deed on social media, it usually comes back to you several-fold. In other words, when you shout them out, they'll return the favor. When you refer customers to them--they'll do the same for you.

Share other people's posts.

This is a fairly easy thing to do on social media platforms like Facebook and Twitter, but on Instagram, the best way to do it is by creating an Instagram Story. You'll see this feature by clicking the icon that looks like an airplane under any post, and then clicking "Add post to your story." Whatever the case, sharing meaningful posts from others is also a great form of engagement. It tells people you're connected to the community and you have no problem promoting other people's stuff. And, you guessed it...they're more likely to start sharing your stuff, too.

Engage specifically with influencers.

Influencers are people who have a large following on social media, typically because of the expertise or niche they fill in the lives of their followers (for example, they might be a fashionista or an expert on surfing or tech). These people are called influencers because they can affect people's buying decisions. They don't necessarily have to be in a field related to yours, but they are incredibly important to your business because if you're able to form a relationship with them, you might be able to get them to promote your services directly or simply introduce people in their audience who might be in the market to buy or sell a home. You may also be able to find creative ways to collaborate with influencers on certain projects or promotions that might be mutually beneficial or even serve the community. Collaborating with an influencer immediately expands your own sphere of influence and puts you in front of a whole new audience.

Now, one point to mention is that many social media influencers end up making a living at it--and even getting wealthy from it--by doing their promotions for pay. This is a highly popular marketing tactic known as "influencer marketing," and businesses often pay thousands of dollars to certain influencers just for them to mention their product or service to their followers. I'm not saying you need to do that (unless you want to and you have the money to spare). But there are other ways to connect with and collaborate with influencers organically, especially if you establish a rapport and if you both have something to gain from the connection.

Developing Social Currency

In my view, one of the best things about this new social media marketing landscape is that success is no longer based on how deep your pockets are. It used to be that the more money you had available to spend on advertising, the more success you had. In the world of social media, we basically use a different kind of currency, one that's based on influence, not affluence. In this world, it's not about how much money you can spend on advertising, but how well you use your social media presence to build credibility and relationships with potential customers. We refer to this idea as social currency.

The idea behind social currency is that businesses are no longer trusted simply because they're known brands. Consumers look to what their friends, family, and the people they follow on social media say about a product before making a purchase decision. When someone shares one of your posts on their own social media, that's a sign that you've built social currency with them. Even more so when they recommend you to their followers after having done business with you. That's your aim here--to develop strong social currency with your following through quality content and consistent engagement.

Alongside your real estate pillar, the Pillar of Content community expert could come in very handy here. Amid your other content, when you post about your local community or the local real estate market, reserve your posts for genuinely helpful information, local recommendations, etc. View yourself as a friend to your followers, especially those in your local community. Be quick to respond to comments, messages, and questions, and always thank people who re-share your content. Doing so makes you accessible and helps to build trust among your followers.

What About Social Media Advertising?

Now, at this point in the discussion, a lot of other books about social media would steer you toward the importance of investing in Facebook ads, Instagram ads, and even Google ads as part of your marketing strategy. It's an inevitable question, but a fair one: Should you do paid social media advertising? Is it worth the investment?

My answer is a guarded "yes." Social media ads do work for most industries--IF you know how to create them and place them. But in my experience, that's a big IF, especially when it comes to real estate brokers or marketing listings online.

The thing about advertising on social media is that it's almost an art form unto itself. Advertising on the Internet in general is not like placing a billboard in a high-traffic area where millions of people are going to drive by and see it every day. With social media ads, the target audience doesn't drive by the billboard--the billboard "drives by" the audience, if you will. The social media algorithm shows the ad to a certain target audience based on the parameters you set when you set up the ad. You set up a budget, and you only pay for the number of clicks you receive.

Sounds easy, right? But there are a few flies in the ointment:

- *First*...figuring out exactly how to set your parameters to reach exactly the right people can be very challenging, and if you don't know how to do it (if you're not a professional Facebook marketer, for example), chances are your ad dollars won't go very far because your reach won't be accurate.

- *Second*...figuring out a good call-to-action on social media ads can be tricky for real estate agents. You're most likely not going to sell a listing with a Facebook or Instagram ad--although you might get a few people to come to an open house if you target locally. Social media ads tend to work best for getting people to *sign up* for something rather than to *buy* something. In other words, they're good for getting people into a sales funnel--but you have to have a clearly defined funnel to make it work.

- *Third*...and this is a big one...although you're paying per click, you're not actually "buying" ad space online. You're *bidding* for it. It's complicated, but social media advertising is more like an auction where the greatest visibility goes to the highest bidders. You're not guaranteed a certain number of clicks when you set up your budget because you're competing with other advertisers for visibility. One digital marketing expert compared the process to poker--only the people with fat wallets are invited to the high-stakes tables.

My point is not to discourage you from advertising on social media or Google. As I said, it does work when it's done right. But if you want to do it, I think your marketing dollars would be better spent hiring a social media marketing company to design and place the ads for you. (See the chapter on "Working with a Social Media Partner" toward the end of the book for more information on that.) For now, it's a better investment of your own time and energy to focus on growing your following organically using the principles I'm teaching you here.

Effective Use of Hashtags

I want to go into a bit more depth about using hashtags because this is one of the most important things you can do to grow your following on Instagram. Hashtags are keywords prefaced with a "#" symbol, and they are a way to make posts searchable according to topic and relevance so people can more easily find those posts and connect with others who share their interests. For example, typing the hashtag *#travel* in Instagram's search bar will show you a collection of posts related to traveling. If you're selling real estate in Canton, Ohio and want to see what people are talking about relating to your city, typing the hashtag *#cantonohio* will deliver you the most popular posts with that hashtag attached to them.

Think of hashtags as your gateway to connect with new like-minded people with whom you don't yet have a connection. All Instagram posts are public, but when you pull up your own Instagram feed, you only see posts from people you're following, and vice versa (with the exception of a few sponsored ads sprinkled in). But if you search for specific hashtags, you'll find posts from people you're not following, and you can follow them, comment, start conversations, and so on. Likewise, when you attach hashtags to your posts, then people who aren't yet connected to you can find your posts using those hashtags and interact with you. (And by the way, hashtags are used across almost every social media platform these days--Twitter was the first to use them--and they work pretty much the same way on each platform.)

There are millions of hashtags in use today, and as you can imagine, using them effectively is a combination of art and science. So let's talk about how to use them to your greatest advantage.

Choosing Which Hashtags to Use

For starters, I recommend compiling a core group of relevant hashtags around each of your Pillars of Content. You can easily find lists of popular hashtags through a basic Google search or even through Instagram's own Search and Explore section. For example, if I Google "Top real estate hashtags," I'll get links to several websites that list some of the most frequently used hashtags around real estate. If I type "realestate" into Instagram's search bar, then tap the "#" icon below it, Instagram will show me the top hashtags containing "realestate" along with how many posts are currently associated with each hashtag.

Plan to spend some time exploring and experimenting with hashtag strings to see what you find. The longer and more specific the hashtag, usually the fewer the posts associated with it. For example, I just typed *#springtime* into Instagram and it shows nearly 19 million posts with that hashtag, while *#springtimeinnyc* has just over 10,000 posts associated with it. Bear in mind that choosing the hashtags with the largest number of posts isn't always better--because you're competing with potentially millions of other posts. What's important is that your hashtags are *relevant* to what you're talking about. Just as with anything else, sometimes a "niche" hashtag with only a few thousand people using it will give you more meaningful connections than one that's used by millions, especially if the hashtag is relevant to what you're posting.

I recommend gathering a collection of hashtags relevant to your real estate pillar--a blend of highly-used and medium-used ones--along with hashtags associated with your local area (e.g., *#tamparealestate, #realestatetampa*) and maybe even hashtags of certain popular neighborhoods where you sell. Get a bunch of these together and save them in a document so you can refer to them later and copy/paste them into your posts. Repeat this process for all your other Pillars of Content.

Where to Place Your Hashtags

There's no shortage of debate as to the best place to put hashtags in the post. Some people put a long string of them right at the end of the post. Some put the hashtags in the comment section of their own post to separate it from the rest of their content. Each school of thought has its own arguments as to why their way is the best.

For the way Instagram currently "reads" data, the best practice for maximum visibility is to include the hashtags somewhere in the body of the post (not in the comments). Most professional pages nowadays will use a line break generator to "push" the hashtags below the line of visibility so viewers can't see them unless they hit the "more" button on your post. Another shortcut for doing this is simply to hit "period-enter" about six or seven times before inserting your hashtags.

Don't Overdo the Hashtags

When Instagram first started implementing hashtags and

people began understanding their power, a lot of people adopted the practice of putting dozens and dozens of hashtags at the end of each of their posts trying to make them as visible as possible. The idea was, of course, that "more is better." Instagram has gotten wise to this practice, so the algorithm has been adjusted so if you overdo the number of hashtags on your post, Instagram just stops indexing it and showing it to people.

In our current experience, my team and I have found that the "sweet spot" for Instagram hashtags is currently around 12-15 per post. Any more than 16-17, and you're probably facing diminishing returns on visibility. I recommend choosing a set of relevant hashtags from the core group of them you've gathered, starting with some of the most often used ones. Then save the last few for local or community-based hashtags or "niche" hashtags.

Use Your Hashtags to Find Others

Remember earlier when I said to make collections of core hashtags for each of your Pillars of Content? Those hashtags aren't just for adding to your posts so people can find you-- they also work in reverse. By typing one of those hashtags into the Search and Explore section, you can find and reach out to lots of other people who are already using that hashtag. (That's basically the same way other people are going to start finding *you* with the hashtags you've added to your posts.) Don't be shy. Spend some quality time searching your own hashtag collections for people who look like they'd be good contacts for you. Comment on their posts. Message them directly if you have something meaningful to say. Don't just sit and wait for people to find you with those hashtags. Reach out and start conversations. Remember, this is all about engagement, and engagement is a two-way street. If you do this only passively, you're not going to see the same results. Be active in your search for new connections, and you'll grow your sphere of influence much faster.

Using Geotags

Finally, let's talk about one other connection point that often gets overlooked--connecting via geotags.

A lot of people confuse hashtags with geotags because of the "tag" thing. They work similarly, but they're not the same. A geotag is like a pinpoint on a map. When you allow your Instagrama app to access your location, the app knows your geographic location when you post on your phone. It then gives you the option to add a geotag to your post (you'll find this option under "Add location"). If none of the suggested locations are correct, you can type in one of your own. When you post it, it is now "tagged" with geographic metadata, and others looking for posts from that location can now find it much the same way that they find you using hashtags. To search for geotagged posts in your area, type in the name of the location in Instagram's search bar, and instead of clicking the "#" icon, tap the icon that looks like a map point.

Geotags can be highly effective for you as a real estate agent particularly when you're sharing information about great neighborhoods or posting about your listings. Adding a geotag can help you make a connection with people who are looking for information about that location, or who may even be shopping for a house there.

Hopefully, as you're working through all this information, you're starting to see the potential for exponential growth, not just for your social media presence but also for your business. Let's talk next about how to tell whether your social media efforts are working and how you can improve your processes.

7. MEASURING YOUR RESULTS

STEVE MARABOLI ONCE SAID, "If you don't know exactly where you are going, how will you know when you get there?"

I'd like to rephrase that idea in my own words: "If you don't know what success looks like, how will you know when you're successful?"

It's all well and good to develop all this great content for social media and spend all this time engaging with people, but at some point in the process (multiple points, in fact), you need to step back and track your progress to see what kind of results you're getting.

This is a basic principle with any marketing strategy. You try something, you measure the results, you tweak it, you revamp it in different ways. You do A/B testing of different versions of an ad, an email, a direct mail piece, to see which version gets you more responses. If something isn't producing results, you make adjustments and try again. If it's still not getting results, maybe you abandon it and try something else.

The concepts I've shared with you thus far are proven techniques to grow your social media following, generate more leads, and ultimately more sales. But implementing those principles is going to work differently for different people, even among real estate agents working in the same market. You shouldn't just put up a bunch of content, spit out a bunch of comments and likes on random posts, and hope for the best. You might get results, you might not. But there's always a way to get *better* results.

And you won't know how to get those better results if you're not measuring your results regularly.

We won't spend too much time on this topic because once you learn your way around the idea of analytics, measuring your progress is pretty self-explanatory. But let me introduce you to some of the basics, including what you need to look at, how to interpret what you're seeing, and tips for making adjustments to your marketing strategy.

Analytics and Insights

The first place to start is your analytics--the numbers that show your activity on social media and what kind of responses you're getting. Every social media platform offers some type of analytics data--much the same way Google Analytics can analyze the activity on your website. Typically, the most in-depth insights are reserved for business pages and accounts. If you have converted your Instagram profile into a professional profile as I recommended back in Chapter 3, you'll have access to these deeper numbers in your "Insights" section. It will show you various analytics such as how many followers and non-followers you're reaching, how many followers you've gained and lost, what kind of engagements you're getting, and specific insights into your posts, Instagram Stories, Reels, etc.

What You Need to Look For

In figuring out whether your social media strategy is working, the main metrics you need to be looking at are the metrics around engagement. Don't just look at the number of followers you have (although if you're doing things right, that number should be growing). Instead, focus on how many likes you're getting per post, how many comments, how many shares. Instagram Stories, Reels, and other video-based content will also show you how many views you're getting, and that's important because it shows you your reach. Again, engagement is one of the biggest drivers of growth. If your content is prompting people to respond, you're going to gain a loyal following and greater levels of influence in your social community. So focus most of your attention on what's happening in the realm of engagement.

Specifically, I'd take a look at the following aspects:

- *Total likes, comments, and shares over a period of time.* Look at it month-to-month, or week-to-week. Is your total number of engagements growing over time, or is it shrinking?
- *Engagements among different types of posts.* If your videos and Stories are performing better than your photos, that's something to look at. If content based on one of your Pillars of Content is doing better or worse than the other pillars, take note of that, too. Start asking why? What's working, and what isn't?
- *Location of engagements.* Insights often show you where people are responding from. Are you seeing mostly engagements from people outside your local area, or inside it? (This is an important number to look at because as a real estate agent, you want a significant number of local responses.)
- *Posts that underperform.* You'll probably be able to identify a few posts that generated fewer engagements or even a dismal number of responses compared to the others. What do these posts share

in common? Why do you think they
underperformed?
- *Posts that do better than others.* What do these posts
share in common? Why do you think they
resonated better?
- *Followers.* Gaining and losing followers is part of
the process. Are you seeing a net gain of followers
over time, or are you seeing more people leave?

Tweaking Your Approach for Maximum Effectiveness

Once you have a grasp of the numbers and what they're telling
you, it's time to figure out what to do about them. Perfecting
any marketing strategy is all about making tweaks--trying
things, then trying different things, making small changes (or
big ones) to maximize your results. The same is true of social
media marketing. It's all about evaluating results and making
course corrections to get better results.

There are basically two guiding principles to follow when
tweaking your approach:

1. *Do more of what's working.* If your videos get more
   engagement than your photos, post some more
   videos. If your Stories are getting lots of traction,
   hone in on this feature and do more Stories. If
   posting on certain days and/or times gets you more
   visibility and engagement, post more on those days
   and at those times.
2. *Fix what's not working.* If you're posting too often
   and it's resulting in poor engagement, tone it
   down and focus a little more on quality than
   quantity. If one of your Pillars of Content is just
   not getting attention, look for ways to revamp the
   content--or if you're just not feeling it anymore,
   remove that pillar from the mix. Analyze the

language of posts that underperform and try changing the tone a bit. If you're not seeing any new followers from certain hashtags, try swapping them out for different ones. You can even try subtler changes like using softer filters or different color schemes for your photos.

This part truly is not an exact science--it's more trial-and-error than anything else. Sometimes finding the ideal mix of content, posting times, hashtag use, etc. is nothing more than alchemy. Keep experimenting until you see better results, then do more of what's working, fix what's not working...and the cycle continues.

The Bigger Picture: Are You Generating Leads?

Of course, all the metrics I mentioned above are only going to measure how well you're doing on social media. But you also need to remember why you're doing this and what your larger goal is. Every so often, you need to look at your actual numbers of real estate leads and sales. Are your efforts on social media resulting in more leads? More revenue? If not, then it's time to look at your overall marketing strategy and start asking yourself some questions. For example:

- Are you posting consistently?
- Is your content high-quality? Does it generate interest?
- Are you spending enough time engaging people?
- Are you establishing yourself as an authority--as an expert on real estate and your local community?
- Are you being authentic?

As you're evaluating your results and contemplating changes, the one thing I would definitely advise against: **Don't**

give up on the whole idea of social media marketing. That's NOT a tweak you should make. Remember what I said at the beginning: if social media isn't working for you, it's not because it doesn't work. It's because you haven't figured out how to make it work for you. There's just too much evidence that this DOES work, and I'm living proof. Everyone's different, and your path to social media success may look a little different than mine. Keep trying. Hire some social media marketing professionals if you need to, but keep at it until you figure out what works for you.

8. A LOOK AT OTHER SOCIAL MEDIA PLATFORMS

WE'VE TALKED at length about how to utilize Instagram because in my view, it's currently the social media platform that offers the greatest benefit to real estate brokers. But it's certainly not the only player in the field--and it's certainly not the only platform *I'm* on. Every platform has a distinct personality, a unique set of advantages, and typically caters to a certain type of person or demographic. I've also mentioned before that the techniques we've discussed using Instagram can be largely adapted to most other social media outlets.

Since most of us have at least a little experience with social media, I'm not going to insult your intelligence by assuming you know nothing about these platforms. But having said that, let's explore a few of these other platforms from the standpoint of marketing your real estate business so you can decide whether they might be worth investigating.

Facebook

I almost feel dumb starting with this one, because...*Facebook*. Everyone knows about this one. Almost half the population of the world has a Facebook account. It's a good solid platform for businesses in general because Facebook offers business pages that are designed to help you connect with customers. Facebook also owns Instagram, so if you're following my advice, I know you probably already have a Facebook page because you can't have an Instagram business account without one.

You can use your Facebook profile to connect with people as a human, or you can set up a Facebook business page, or you can have both. (I have both.) You'll find many of the same features on Facebook as on Instagram, including Stories, Reels, and Facebook Live. Facebook also has Facebook Groups which can be very useful for real estate brokers in several ways. You can join existing groups around real estate or your other Pillars of Content and enter into meaningful discussions there--or you can set up your own Facebook groups to facilitate discussions with your own following. Facebook began mostly as a college crowd, but nowadays, much of the younger crowd has migrated off of Facebook for other platforms, and many of the regular users are in the 40-and-up demographic.

Twitter

This is another platform almost everyone knows about--and many thought it would overtake Facebook at one time. But today, it's actually one of the lesser-used platforms with only around 200 million active users. Twitter is all about short "tweets"--there's a 280-character maximum per tweet. You can also share photos, articles, videos, etc. on the platform. It works well as a platform for sharing breaking news tidbits or short bursts of information, but not necessarily image-heavy or video-driven content.

LinkedIn

LinkedIn is, for all intents and purposes, the social media platform for business professionals. It's all about connecting
around business-related issues. It has also become one of the
primary tools for job seekers; there's a whole jobs section to it,
and for many people, their LinkedIn profile doubles as their
resume. LinkedIn also has a Company Pages feature, but in
my experience, most people focus their energies on their
personal profiles and networking with other professionals.

For real estate brokers, LinkedIn can be particularly useful
in a couple of ways. First, it's a great place to form connections
with other brokers and other business professionals, either as
potential customers or for referrals. Second, LinkedIn has
become a popular place to post informative articles, so a lot of
people use that feature to post longer-form content to demon-
strate their expertise and build credibility within their industry. One other thing you should know about LinkedIn: It's an
SEO powerhouse. It always ranks super-high on the search
engines, so having content up on LinkedIn is a great way for
people to discover you by Googling topics in your area of
expertise.

YouTube

Part-search engine, part social media platform, and mostly-
video hosting site, YouTube is no doubt one of the busiest
places on the web. As a search engine, it's second in size only
to Google (who happens to own it). As a social media site, it's
second in size only to Facebook with more than 2 billion
users--even though most people probably don't even think of
it as a social media platform, but rather just as a place to host
and watch videos. It's got all the basic elements of social media
except with slightly different terminology (your profile is your
"channel," for example, and followers are "subscribers"), and

you can even like and comment on videos. Many people have used YouTube to amass huge followings by posting entertaining or informative videos, and because YouTube shares advertising revenue with users with big followings and large numbers of views, a lot of "YouTube stars" have made it their primary source of income.

As a real estate broker, unless you have an idea to build your entire following around videos, chances are YouTube won't be your primary platform. However, I do see it as an essential supplementary platform, especially if you intend to incorporate video with your content as I've recommended.

Snapchat

A few years ago, Snapchat was the rage among the under-25 set, basically gearing its entire approach around immediacy and posting short video clips that disappear after a day. (Instagram basically "borrowed" this concept for its Instagram Stories feature.) Today, Snapchat has a much lower profile than it used to. However, almost two-thirds of twenty-somethings still use it, so it might be useful to brokers who want to reach first-time homebuyers. For what it's worth, though, Instagram Stories does basically the same thing, and it even lets you save your Stories as Highlights, which Snapchat does not do.

TikTok

Originally emerging as a place for people to post snappy, super-fun, short videos of themselves dancing, TikTok has grown to be one of the hottest new platforms on the web. Unlike Snapchat, the videos on TikTok don't go away, and the platform now allows videos of up to two minutes. A lot of people still assume it's mainly a hangout for teenagers, but the reality is that TikTok now has users from a wide swath of age brackets posting videos of all kinds. Instagram developed its Reels feature to compete with this format (hey, I said Instagram was *good*, not that it was always *original*), so if these snappy short videos are a good fit for you, you might be happy enough just using Instagram. However, TikTok supports a lot of users who don't use Instagram regularly--including a lot of potential home buyers and sellers. So don't write this one off-- it might be worth having a supplemental presence there.

This is just a cross-section of some of the more popular social media sites out there. There are others, of course, and there will likely be new ones that show up after this book has been published. Bear in mind that you don't need to have an account on every social media outlet, and if you did, it would be nearly impossible to keep up with all of them regularly. Most people who are successfully branding themselves on social media (including real estate agents) will typically find 3-4 platforms that are a good fit for their personality as well as their target market, and their marketing strategy will focus on those platforms. For me, I use Instagram as my primary, but I'm also regularly on Facebook, LinkedIn, YouTube, and TikTok. You might choose a different set of platforms, and you might even prefer a different platform as your main go-to (Facebook, for example). Whatever works for you is ultimately fine as long as you post consistently, engage regularly, and keep your content compelling.

One final tip before we move on: Whatever platforms you choose, make sure you're posting original content on all of them--don't repost the exact same post on Instagram, Facebook, Twitter, etc. Change up the language, re-edit the videos, space out the timing of your posts between platforms, and so on. The reason is that many of your followers will be following you on multiple platforms, and copying posts across platforms can get repetitive to them, even annoying. Try to organize your posts in a way that people feel your content is always fresh wherever they happen to find you.

9. MAKING SOCIAL MEDIA PART OF YOUR BRAND

BY THIS POINT, you have basically all the concepts in place to develop a powerful social media presence for marketing your real estate business. As we come near the end of our discussion, let's step back and look again at the bigger picture. Looking at all the elements of your various social media platforms--from your photos and videos to your conversations--what is the thread that ties everything together? How do you design your social media presence so that everything about it is consistent, reflecting your personality and that of your business? How do you make it all...*you?*

This is where the idea of *branding* comes in.

The concept of branding is actually thousands of years old. It's derived from the ancient practice of livestock owners who would take a firebrand and burn their unique mark of ownership onto their livestock so their animals could be identified and wouldn't get mixed up with their neighbor's livestock. Today, the concept of branding in business is similar, except that we're trying to "burn" a mental imprint of our company into the minds of the public so they can easily identify us. We do this by trying to create consistent experiences and associations every time someone comes in contact with our business. Color schemes, logos, jingles, sounds, and sometimes even smells (food companies, for example) can become part of our brand.

Developing Your Brand on Social Media

When we carry the idea of branding into social media, we view each post and interaction as an opportunity to build our brand. This means that every social media platform you use should be aligned with your business's other materials and branding elements. It also means that you strive to have all your content maintain a distinctive look and feel to it--a "vibe," if you will--that is uniquely yours. The goal is for people to immediately recognize you or your business from the content itself even before they see or hear your name.

I can't tell you exactly how to design and develop this "vibe." You have to make those decisions yourself. What I can tell you is that effective branding takes time and patience, and your brand will evolve through trial and error. As you experiment with different types of posts and content, you'll develop a sense of what works for you and what doesn't. Over time, you'll begin to identify through your own experience which colors are most effective, which kinds of images resonate the most with people, and so on.

Because we're approaching social media as a marketing tool--often used in conjunction with other marketing methods--chances are you have already started working on branding yourself as a real estate broker. If you've done any mass advertising, mailers, and the like, you are likely already on this path. When you add social media to the mix, it's just a matter of translating the existing elements of your brand into your social media presence--to make your profiles, posts, and engagements recognizable and consistent with your other branded materials.

But I'd recommend taking this idea a step further. Instead of merely seeing social media as one more outlet for your branding, I want you to consider making *social media itself* part of your brand.

In other words, you're not just known around town because you have effectively used social media to spread your message. You're known around town as the "social media agent." Your brand becomes so indelibly associated with social media that people know that's where they can find you when they want you.

This is the approach I've chosen with my own real estate brokerage, and it has amplified my results more than you can imagine. It's become part of my Unique Selling Proposition. People looking to sell homes in NYC now seek me out because they know I'm good at social media, and because I know how to use social media and professionally produced videos to get their listings in front of tens of thousands of excited potential buyers. People looking to buy in NYC seek me out because they saw my listings on their social media feeds--or because they just remember me from social media. Leveraging social media has become an identifying marker for my business, and it differentiates me from other agents in my area. It's become my niche, so to speak.

But I'm not the only one who's done this--nor should I be the only one. The social media landscape is vast, and there's plenty of room for up-and-coming brokers and agents to establish their own brands in unique and creative ways. As I said at the beginning, I believe social media is the new marketing landscape. It's continuing to gain relevance even as other marketing tools are becoming more ineffective. Most importantly, as a broker, most of your target market is hanging out on social media just waiting for you to connect with them and establish yourself as someone to trust.

Social media is too old now to be a fad, and it's a long way from becoming obsolete. There's still a lot of wide-open space here. Real estate agents who are forward-thinking enough to stake their claim early within this new landscape--these are the ones who stand to make millions while building a long and productive career.

10. WORKING WITH A SOCIAL MEDIA PARTNER

AS YOU CONSISTENTLY APPLY THE techniques and principles I've shared with you in this book, you *will* start seeing results. Your following will grow, your engagement with them will grow--and so will your level of trust. Some of these followers will become leads, and some of them will become clients--and then those clients will become your cheerleaders, sharing your content with others.

The concepts in this book are designed so that you can get started with social media marketing with little or no cash outlay. But as I've said before, it does require a time commitment to make it work. That's one of the reasons I've also recommended that you re-think your marketing approach and focus most of your marketing time, energy, and resources toward social media. I'm not saying to do only social media and eliminate your website, newsletter, ad campaigns, etc. (As I said, I still do those things, too.) It's a matter of prioritizing your time and resources into what works. Social media marketing works when you put the time in--and you'll soon see that you are okay spending more time (and money) on Instagram and less time (and money) on other marketing tactics that are no longer producing the same kinds of results.

All that said, if you do this right, you're likely going to hit a tipping point. Your social media presence is going to grow, and the more it grows, the more attention it's going to need. You'll also feel the need to "up your game" as far as your content goes. Those homemade videos might start looking a bit shabby to you--and truth be told, once your following reaches a certain level, there's an expectation of professionalism that comes with that new territory. These are good growing pains to have, but time now becomes a challenge.

And let's be honest--some people just don't feel they have the time to devote to making social media work the way they want it to, even some who are just getting started. Maybe for you, real estate is a side gig that you hope will turn into your full-time gig, and maybe your "day job" takes too much time out of your day. Or maybe you're a single parent with little ones at home, and they take up a lot of your attention after hours. Maybe you're convinced by now that you could make your real estate business explode with social media marketing, but the time requirement puts it just out of reach.

In either case--whether you're struggling with time commitments or whether you've reached that "tipping point" of growth--it may be time for you to consider working with a social media partner.

Now, to be clear, hiring a social media agency doesn't just mean you're going to pay them a bunch of money to handle all your accounts for you. That's not quite how it works. But what working with an agency *will* do is give you a powerful support system--a team of experts and professionals who can do a lot of the heavy lifting for you. If social media is a ship, you're still the captain, and you're the one who sets the course and calls the shots. You've just brought on a top-notch crew so you don't have to handle all the responsibilities yourself. You'll still come up with ideas for content, and you'll still handle a lot of your own engagement with your followers. But you won't be doing it alone--

and in fact, your team will lend expertise that can really take your social media presence to the next level, ultimately resulting in profits that far exceed what you've invested for the help.

I established my own social media company, Very Social, specifically because I saw the potential of social media for real estate agents and wanted to help them replicate my success at it. We serve clients from a variety of industries, but the majority of our clients are real estate agents--and since I'm a broker myself, we're an especially good fit for the needs of agents and brokers. We've assembled a team of extremely talented graphic designers, copywriters, and marketing/branding experts who know how to create content that builds interest. Every agency does things a little bit differently, but here's a rundown of what we do:

- We strategize with you to identify and develop your Pillars of Content
- We help you create a content strategy and posting plan around those Pillars of Content, collaborating with you on the posting schedule (typically a month in advance)
- We employ our graphic designers and copywriters to develop the content for/with you
- We do the physical posting on your social media accounts according to the schedule we've developed
- We do regular audits of your social media accounts to look at content and engagement, we recommend tweaks to get better results
- We develop and execute highly effective social media advertising campaigns for our clients who want to do paid ads
- For clients who desire it, we also have an influencer marketing department that helps our clients hire

and/or collaborate with known social media
influencers

In short, for virtually all the principles and techniques I've shared with you in this book, Very Social gives you the support of a team of experts who have proven success with these processes, along with a dedicated account manager who coordinates all the moving pieces for you.

Now, let's be absolutely clear: You don't *need* my social media agency to be successful in social media marketing. You really can do it all by yourself by implementing the things I've taught you here--and if you do them, you'll succeed, and that's great! But if you're in a position where you want some help taking things to the next level, it's well worth the investment to hire a social media partner, whether it's Very Social or some other reputable agency you know. And while you absolutely can see your real estate revenues soar just by doing the things I've recommended, hiring a team at the right time can also amplify your results exponentially, even beyond your wildest dreams.

Whatever the case, just know that you're not alone on this journey. There are people who have successfully walked this road before you, and help is available if you need it. Check out the contact information at the end of the book to reach out to us.

BONUS SECTION: 100 IDEAS FOR SOCIAL MEDIA CONTENT

As we talked about back in Chapter 4, one of the keys to a powerful social media presence is to post excellent consistent content. However, sometimes it's easier said than done, especially if you don't know WHAT to post or how to engage people. As a bonus and a "thank you" for reading this book, I'm including 100 inspiration ideas for coming up with great content. I've used all of these ideas at one time or another, and they've always helped me stay on track. Refer back to this list again and again every time you feel stuck, and you should never experience "writer's block" with your social media again.

1. Announce new listings
2. Do liveaways (e.g., merch, gift cards to local restaurants, etc.)
3. Contests (great way to engage an audience)
4. Helpful news or information
5. Profile or shout-out other local businesses
6. Humorous posts (share funny stuff you come across)
7. Real estate tips (e.g., how to stage your home for showing, tips for picking a neighborhood)

8. Videos of home tours
9. Home of the Week (profile an awesome home in the area—doesn't even have to be your listing)
10. Client testimonials
11. Day-In-The-Life videos (what you do during a "normal" day)
12. Polls (great engagement tool)
13. Video series (get creative with topics or themes)
14. Serving the community (highlight causes you support, encourage volunteerism, etc.)
15. Highlights—invite followers to check out some of your Instagram highlights
16. Behind-The-Scene (BTS) videos
17. Fun facts (could be on real estate market or anything else)
18. Question and Answer (pick a commonly asked question about you or your brokerage and answer it)
19. Partnership or business spotlight (businesses you work with)
20. Lighthearted posts (e.g., family, favorite spots)
21. How-To lists
22. IY tips
23. Real estate expert advice
24. Client events
25. Closing post (letting people know when you've completed a sale)
26. Holiday messages
27. Share memes
28. Housing market info
29. Pet bio—talk about your pet(s) and share photos
30. Personal posts
31. Open House announcements
32. Throwback Thursday posts (#TBT, pick a popular post from your previous ones and re-post it)

33. Anniversary of the sale/purchase of a home—if the home itself or circumstances surrounding the sale are noteworthy, it's a great time to reintroduce the home
34. Client appreciation
35. Astrology post (e.g., tell them your sign, ask them what their sign is, etc.)
36. Employee Spotlight
37. Social Media Holidays (e.g., National Pizza Day, Teacher Appreciation Week...do a Google search for some great ideas)
38. Your most expensive listing
39. Team birthdays
40. Buying goals (e.g., your goal for the month/year for number of buyers you help to find a home)
41. Selling goals (e.g., your goal for the month/year for number of home sales you facilitate)
42. My biggest real estate lesson (an experience that taught you something important)
43. Why your team is different
44. Thank You (to your followers, or anyone else you think of)
45. Blog posts (link to blogs you've written or other people's blogs)
46. What is your passion? (invite followers to share their passions, hobbies, etc.)
47. Local market listings
48. Company news
49. Company events
50. Your own home—share photos, stories, etc.
51. Interior design inspiration
52. Content creation—behind the scenes (BTS)
53. Tips for buyers
54. Tips for sellers
55. Rent vs Own

56. Mortgage info
57. Why work with me?
58. Neighborhood Guides
59. My favorite spots in _____
60. Before/After renovations
61. Carousel photos of a property tour
62. Community Aid Day: Take a day to do something active for your community, whether it's packing meals for the houseless, raking leaves for the elderly, etc. Take photos of your team at work, or do a video interview with someone in the neighborhood. Include a call to action for followers to get active in the community.
63. Outdoor Space of the Week (highlight gardens, great backyard spaces, etc.)
64. AMA (ask me anything)—invite followers to pose questions, then answer them
65. Cross promotions with partner businesses or other influencers
66. Free resources
67. Real estate milestones
68. Ask for feedback on stagings
69. Seasonal home decorating tips
70. Current discounts and Special Offers
71. Repost content from local experts
72. National industry news
73. Historical pictures of your area
74. Latest home tech
75. What NOT to buy
76. Showcase your hobbies
77. New constructions
78. Personal Branding—plan a series of posts that help tell your personal story and give followers a better sense of your brand
79. Housing trends

80. Recreation activities in your area
81. Dog-friendly spots in your area
82. Kid-friendly spots in your area
83. Home maintenance advice
84. Relocation information (moving to ___? Here's what you need to know)
85. Share your story
86. Local getaways
87. Service recommendations—highlight or shout-out a local service or company that has done good work for you
88. Home decor
89. Design Style This-Or-That (post two pics and ask followers to choose a favorite)
90. Pet showcase (invite followers to share photos of their pets)
91. Two Truths and a Lie (make three statements about yourself, your brokerage, etc., and invite followers to pick out the lie)
92. Document a local event (think Festival, Concert, Block Party)
93. Showcase your expertise through storytelling
94. State and local facts
95. Time-lapse video to showcase event or property
96. Favorite local bites and restaurants
97. Best outdoor dining
98. How I got into real estate
99. Best local hikes or walks
100. Drone footage to highlight unique or hard-to-capture scenes and listings

AFTERWORD

And so we come to the end. Or actually, the beginning.

The concepts we've talked about in this book came out of a long personal journey. No one really taught me these things--some things I learned from plain old trial-and-error, other things I picked up from others as I went along. But you're just beginning your social media adventure, and my hope in sharing these things is that your path to success will be smoother and faster because you'll have avoided some of the mistakes I made.

Speaking of which--just know that you're *going to make mistakes*. You're going to try some things that fall flat. You're probably going to encounter some frustration along the way. Don't despair when it happens--it's part of the learning process. Learn from your mistakes, change your tactics, and keep moving forward. Social media mastery is a process, and even though your journey should go easier from the things I've shared here, you still need to be patient with yourself through the process. Consistency is key--not just in what you post or how often, but in sticking with it. The only way you'll fail is if you quit.

I recommend that you hang on to this book and revisit it

every time you need a refresher or a bit of encouragement.
Review the Pillars of Content chapter when you're struggling
to figure out what to post. If your following isn't growing as it
should, re-read "Expanding Your Audience--and Your Influence" to make sure you're covering all the bases for successful
engagement.

Also, remember that social media is an ever-changing land-
scape--always evolving--but the principles that drive it are
pretty much the same. If in a few years you find your target
audience is dropping off of Instagram for some new social
media platform that didn't exist when you picked up this
book--review the principles and see how you can adapt them
for the new platform. You'll be surprised at how well they still
work.

I'd like to leave you now with five last bits of advice. If you
feel yourself floundering, remember these five things and
you'll do just fine:

1. *Engagement is everything.* Social media is an
   ongoing conversation. Don't just "broadcast." Be
   part of the conversation, and eventually, you can
   even steer the conversation.
2. *Social media is a marathon, not a sprint.* Be
   suspicious of any tactic that promises to instantly
   turn you into a social media star. You might
   experience *quick* growth, but not *lasting* growth--
   and most of the platforms are getting wise to those
   hacks, anyway. The best growth for your brokerage
   is organic. Organic growth lasts.
3. *Tell a story.* We are a people who thrive on stories.
   That's why video works so well with social media--
   it's great for storytelling. Tell the stories behind
   your listings and your successes. When you post
   personal stuff, think of it as telling your ongoing
   story. Make storytelling a guiding principle behind

the content you create, and people will gravitate to
it naturally.

4. *Practice makes perfect.* Trial-and-error is a huge part
   of this process--if you're not making mistakes,
   you're probably doing it wrong! Learn from what
   didn't work in the past so that you can improve
   your future posts. **And keep at it.** I can't stress this
   enough.

5. *Have fun with it!* Be creative. Play. Explore.
   Experiment. Fail, and try again. If you're not
   enjoying the process, what's the point?

Thank you for taking the time to read this book. I truly
hope in the process you've uncovered some inspiration to help
your real estate brokerage grow exponentially. You can do it! I
believe in you. Best of luck on your journey.

NOTES

1. Your New Secret Weapon

1. Justas Gaubys, "How Many People Use Social Media in 2021 [UPDATED Jan 2021]," Oberlo (Oberlo), accessed August 15, 2021, https://www.oberlo.com/statistics/how-many-people-use-social-media
2. "36 Essential Social Media MARKETING Statistics to Know for 2021," Sprout Social, August 17, 2021, https://sproutsocial.com/insights/social-media-statistics/
3. Demographics of Social Media Users and Adoption in the United States," Pew Research Center: Internet, Science & Tech (Pew Research Center, April 26, 2021), https://www.pewresearch.org/internet/fact-sheet/social-media/
4. https://www.pewresearch.org/internet/2021/04/07/social-media-use-in-2021/

4. Developing Your Pillars of Content

1. Thanks to Lance Pendleton, Head of Agent Development at Compass, for introducing me to the concept of mindshare as a way of connecting with people through social media.

ABOUT THE AUTHOR

As a lifetime entrepreneur and natural-born deal maker, Ryan Garson paid his way through college by running a successful events business. By his early twenties, he had turned his South Florida retail company into a national franchise. After moving to New York City at age 30, Ryan became an influential real estate broker covering the boroughs of Manhattan and Brooklyn. Having learned the power of social media marketing early in his career, Ryan contracted over $300 million in sales within his first six years as a broker using social media as his primary tool.

Today, Ryan is known in the industry for his creative, out-of-the-box approach to marketing, combining the latest technologies with targeted, cutting-edge strategies to connect sellers with the right buyers with remarkable efficiency and results. He is also the co-founder and CEO of Very Social, a dynamic social media agency specializing in building and amplifying the brands of real estate professionals and entrepreneurs nationwide.

A firm believer in community involvement, Ryan also serves on the Board of NYC's Garment District, is one of the founding members of the Anti-Defamation League's NY Next Generation Real Estate Group, and is on the Executive Board of the 14th Street YMCA.

Ryan lives in Manhattan with his wife and daughter.